CAMBRIDGE LIBRARY COLLECTION

Books of enduring scholarly value

Spiritualism and Esoteric Knowledge

Magic, superstition, the occult sciences and esoteric knowledge appear regularly in the history of ideas alongside more established academic disciplines such as philosophy, natural history and theology. Particularly fascinating are periods of rapid scientific advances such as the Renaissance or the nineteenth century which also see a burgeoning of interest in the paranormal among the educated elite. This series provides primary texts and secondary sources for social historians and cultural anthropologists working in these areas, and all who wish for a wider understanding of the diverse intellectual and spiritual movements that formed a backdrop to the academic and political achievements of their day. It ranges from works on Babylonian and Jewish magic in the ancient world, through studies of sixteenth-century topics such as Cornelius Agrippa and the rapid spread of Rosicrucianism, to nineteenth-century publications by Sir Walter Scott and Sir Arthur Conan Doyle. Subjects include astrology, mesmerism, spiritualism, theosophy, clairvoyance, and ghost-seeing, as described both by their adherents and by sceptics.

That Other World

Although Stuart Cumberland (1857–1922) was renowned for his mind-reading skills, he was a staunch critic of related spiritualist practices. He claimed that many séances and other events that he had seen confirmed his suspicions that 'the chief basis of the movement was money-making'. So he decided to launch his own campaign to uncover the truth about the methods of spirit-mediums, and in this work, published in 1918, he explains many mediums' tricks, such as making tables move using special silk thread, not spiritual aid. He lectured about the subject in places ranging from Cambridge University to Lambeth Palace, and attributed his own success to his ability to read muscle movement, rather than any supernatural communication. Providing a fascinating picture of the changing spiritualist movement, this work illustrates the extent of the social and political influence of some spiritualists, but also how credibility about their practices was being challenged.

T0381765

Cambridge University Press has long been a pioneer in the reissuing of out-of-print titles from its own backlist, producing digital reprints of books that are still sought after by scholars and students but could not be reprinted economically using traditional technology. The Cambridge Library Collection extends this activity to a wider range of books which are still of importance to researchers and professionals, either for the source material they contain, or as landmarks in the history of their academic discipline.

Drawing from the world-renowned collections in the Cambridge University Library, and guided by the advice of experts in each subject area, Cambridge University Press is using state-of-the-art scanning machines in its own Printing House to capture the content of each book selected for inclusion. The files are processed to give a consistently clear, crisp image, and the books finished to the high quality standard for which the Press is recognised around the world. The latest print-on-demand technology ensures that the books will remain available indefinitely, and that orders for single or multiple copies can quickly be supplied.

The Cambridge Library Collection will bring back to life books of enduring scholarly value (including out-of-copyright works originally issued by other publishers) across a wide range of disciplines in the humanities and social sciences and in science and technology.

That Other World

*Personal Experiences of
Mystics and Their Mysticism*

STUART C. CUMBERLAND

CAMBRIDGE
UNIVERSITY PRESS

CAMBRIDGE UNIVERSITY PRESS

Cambridge, New York, Melbourne, Madrid, Cape Town,
Singapore, São Paolo, Delhi, Tokyo, Mexico City

Published in the United States of America by Cambridge University Press, New York

www.cambridge.org
Information on this title: www.cambridge.org/9781108028516

© in this compilation Cambridge University Press 2011

This edition first published 1918
This digitally printed version 2011

ISBN 978-1-108-02851-6 Paperback

THAT OTHER WORLD

THAT OTHER WORLD

PERSONAL EXPERIENCES OF MYSTICS
AND THEIR MYSTICISM

BY

STUART CUMBERLAND

LONDON
GRANT RICHARDS LTD
ST MARTIN'S STREET
1918

CONTENTS

CHAPTER I

How came I to be first interested in the so-called occult?

Everything has a beginning; and my interest in the mysterious and the phenomena associated with what were then termed " unknown forces " early attracted my attention. Scotch connections had told me of uncanny experiences associated with what was designated as " second sight." More than one claimed to have this gift or to know someone who had it. It was, moreover, a gift that I too might possess. In my youth I dreamt of all kinds of wonderful things I should be able to see and foretell. At that period one possesses much enthusiasm, a high imagination, and precious little logic and power of analysis. Experience alone enables one to weigh, analyse, and discriminate with any approach to accuracy. And this experience I certainly have had.

When spiritualism became a subject of general inquiry I was an early inquirer; and, in an amateurish sort of way, sat with friends seeking for the signs which were said to come to those who sought them in the proper spirit and under congenial conditions.

I entered upon the inquiry not only with a perfectly open mind, but with not a little expectancy. For I had been told of occurrences which were certainly remarkable, and, upon generally accepted principles, quite inexplicable.   But I was soon to learn that things seldom, if ever, occur exactly as related.   What was said to have occurred elsewhere did not occur under the conditions described at sittings I attended.   Indeed, nothing for which a spiritual origin could with any degree of certainty be claimed ever really happened.   The things that did occur seemed to me to come from within the sitters themselves, and that it was unreasoning expectancy that ascribed a supernatural origin to them.   I early saw that not only were the most earnest and veracious people liable to be self-deceived, but that they found comfort in the self-deception.   For, although I may not have inherited the seer's gifts of second sight and so forth, the good gods have endowed me with a certain clearness of vision and a becoming quantity of sound common sense.

The little private séances I attended having produced but negative results, I was induced to pursue my inquiries at sittings where the spirit-controlling genius was a medium of alleged wide experience and great gifts.

From medium to medium I went, to find that the chief basis of the movement was money-making, and that whatever happened there was the outcome of human agency pure and simple, actual spiritual force or influence at such séances having no existence.   Whatever illusions may have remained to me were knocked on the head. Disgust at the chicanery practised and contempt for the puerile manifestations claimed to be spiritual took the place of expectancy and earnest longing for truth. I had indeed arrived at the truth, but through methods which, at the commencement of my investigations, would have been unthinkable.

But it was one thing to put one's personal experience in the scale and, from that experience, to denounce the whole thing as a delusion and a fraud, and another to prove by practical demonstration the real nature and character of the manifestations I myself had witnessed. To duplicate what was duplicable under precisely the same conditions as those under which they were presented as instances of genuine spirit force was the one way to bring the *exposé* home to those who were really desirous of arriving at a correct conclusion on the subject.

And so I set to work not only to find out how the so-called spirit phenomena were produced, but to reproduce them after the manner and under the conditions governing the medium's productions.

I succeeded in enlisting the attention and the support of such really scientific authorities as Charlton Bastian, Crichton-Browne, Lauder Brunton, Brudenell Carter, David Ferrar, Hughlings Jackson, Ray Lankester, Croom Robertson, Huxley, and Tyndall.

Ray Lankester, with the recollection of the impostures perpetrated by the notorious medium Dr Slade, whom he in conjunction with his friend

Horatio Donkin so completely exposed, wrote me the following letter :—

"Having had the opportunity of witnessing your demonstrations of the mode in which so-called spirit-mediums perform the tricks by which they attempt to impose upon the public, I have great pleasure in saying that I have no doubt that you have actually discovered the methods used by those persons, and that your lectures furnish a complete and thorough explanation of the pretended marvels by which many men and women have been cruelly deceived and swindled. I consider that your lectures are likely to do a great deal of good in showing in a convincing manner to those who attend them, how simply the judgment may be misled and erroneous conclusions formed when skilful fraud operates upon credulous ignorance. You have my best wishes for your success in what is, in my opinion, an important EDUCATIONAL enterprise."

Having succeeded in securing the endorsation of most of those who really counted in the scientific world in London, I bethought myself of enlisting the attention of the University authorities of Oxford and Cambridge.

The following attestation I received from the Oxford authorities speaks for itself :—

To STUART C. CUMBERLAND, ESQ.

DEAR SIR,—We have heard with pleasure of your success in exposing the devices of "Spiritualism," and of the satisfactory results you have already achieved in dispelling popular delusions on the subject. From what we have seen ourselves, as well as from the evidence of many competent witnesses, we have no doubt of your skill in producing, by explicable, natural means, the phenomena ascribed to "Spirit-power"; and we are glad to hear of your intention to give in Oxford a private exposition on the subject, which we think may be really useful.

(Signed by)

B. JOWETT, M.A., D.D., Master of Balliol, Professor of Greek, Vice-Chancellor.

T. H. GREEN, M.A., Fellow of Balliol, Professor of Moral Philosophy.

R. B. CLIFTON, M.A., F.R.S., Fellow of Merton, Professor of Experimental Philosophy.

WM. STUBBS, D.D., Fellow of Oriel, Canon of St. Paul's, Regius Professor of Modern History, etc.

WILLIAM ODLING, M.A., F.R.S., Fellow of Worcester, Professor of Chemistry, etc.

C. PRITCHARD, D.D., F.R.S., F.G.S., Professor of Astronomy.

HENRY J. S. SMITH, M.A., F.R.S., Fellow of Balliol, Professor of Geometry, etc.

BARTHOLOMEW PRICE, M.A., F.R.S., Fellow of Pembroke, Professor of Natural Philosophy.

JOSEPH PRESTWICH, M.A., F.R.S., F.G.S., Professor of Geology.

J. LEGGE, M.A., LL.D., Professor of Chinese.

F. MAX MÜLLER, Fellow of All Souls, Professor of Comparative Philology, etc.

E. J. STONE, M.A., F.R.S., Radcliffe Observer.

HY. W. ACLAND, M.D., F.R.S., D.C.L., LL.D., Regius Professor of Medicine, etc.

W. W. MERRY, M.A., Fellow of Lincoln, Public Orator.

H. G. LIDDELL, D.D., Dean of Christ Church, Chaplain Extraordinary to the Queen.

M. A. LAWSON, M.A., F.L.S., Professor of Botany and Rural Economy.

MONIER WILLIAMS, M.A., C.I.E., D.C.L., LL.D., Professor of Sanskrit.

THOMAS FOWLER, M.A., Fellow of Lincoln, Professor of Logic.

J. O. WESTWOOD, M.A., Hon. Fellow of Magdalen, F.A.S., F.L.S., Professor of Zoology.

EDWIN PALMER, D.D., Canon of Christ Church, Archdeacon of Oxford, etc.

EDWIN KING, D.D., Canon of Christ Church, Professor of Pastoral Theology.

C. A. Heurtley, D.D., Canon of Christ Church, Margaret Professor of Divinity.

E. Ray Lankester, M.A., F.R.S., F.L.S., Fellow of Exeter, Professor in University College, London.

W. Markby, M.A., D.C.L., Reader in Indian Law, late Judge Supreme Court of Calcutta.

William Esson, M.A., F.R.S., Fellow and Tutor of Merton.

For the purpose of this private demonstration the hall of Christ Church College was kindly placed at my disposal, and Sir George Sitwell—fresh from his *exposé* of the medium, Florrie Colner, who had succeeded in so completely bamboozling Sir William Crookes—gave me able assistance on the platform.

I afterwards went to Cambridge, under the moral support of the following eminent University authorities :—

James Porter, D.D., Master of St Peter's College, Vice-Chancellor.

W. H. Thompson, D.D., Master of Trinity College.

Charles Taylor, D.D., Master of St John's College.

Richard Okes, D.D., Provost of King's College.

George Phillips, D.D., President of Queens' College.

Robert Phelps, D.D., Master of Sidney-Sussex College.

Thomas Worsley, D.D., Master of Downing College.

B. H. Kennedy, D.D., Regius Professor of Greek, Fellow of St John's, Canon of Ely.

W. Wright, D.D., LL.D., Ph.D., Professor of Arabic, Fellow of Queens'.

G. G. Stokes, M.A., D.C.L., F.R.S., Professor of Mathematics, President of Pembroke, Secretary of Royal Society, etc. etc.

G. M. Humphrey, M.D., F.R.S., Professor of Anatomy, Fellow of Downing.

G. E. Paget, M.D., LL.D., F.R.S., Regius Professor of Medicine, Fellow of Caius.

E. H. Palmer, M.A., Lord Almoner's Professor of Arabic, Fellow of St John's.

J. C. ADAMS, M.A., LL.D., F.R.S., F.R.A.S., Professor of Astronomy, Fellow of Pembroke.

J. A. LUMBY, D.D., Professor of Divinity, Dean of St Catharine's.

P. W. LATHAM, M.D., Downing Professor of Medicine.

W. J. LEWIS, M.A., Professor of Mineralogy.

W. W. SKEAT, M.A., Professor of Anglo-Saxon.

Closely following this, there was held the Church Congress at Newcastle, when one of the chief items of the programme was a discussion dealing with the question of the " Duty of the Church towards Spiritualism and Infidelity."

Despite my extreme youth—for I was by far the youngest speaker there—I was permitted to address the immense audience overflowing the great Town Hall. The reception I received highly gratified me, and I was encouraged to give public meetings with practical demonstrations of the manifestations, passed off as spiritual, and accepted by the credulous as such, all over the country.

In my crusade against the pernicious craze and the vulgar impostures associated with it, I received, in addition to scientific approval, the cordial support of the leading dignitaries of the Church.

The Archbishop of Canterbury (Dr Tait) was good enough to invite me to breakfast at Lambeth Palace, where afterwards I had the privilege of giving some illustrations of the way in which " spirit " phenomena were produced. The present Archbishop was one of the company ; and with him I illustrated the fallacy of Zollner's contention of the existence of a " Fourth Dimension of Space." Of this form of spirit belief, consisting of the passage of matter through matter, I speak in the chapter bearing upon this phenomenon.

I found everywhere a hearty support amongst those of light and leading who really counted, and the common-sense public was unquestionably with me.

A more deeply religious and earnest man than the late Earl of Shaftesbury probably did not exist ; and this is what he said, as chairman, in moving a vote of thanks to me at the conclusion of one of my public representations :—

"I am sure no one will deny that we have had an evening of great amusement and instruction, and, as such, we are deeply indebted to Mr Cumberland.

"The mental and physical powers of Mr Cumberland are simply wonderful, and I certainly am both surprised and delighted at the really marvellous things he has shown us.

"If there had been any doubt in my mind, before coming here, as to the utter humbug of this spiritualistic quackery, I must confess that it would have been at once removed by the clear and thorough *exposé* which our friend has given us.

"I think it a great thing that a gentleman of such ability and such gifts should be found willing to come forward and lay bare the shams of a craze which is harmful to the last degree."

With the approval and support—as I may put it—of all sane and right-thinking people, what mattered the disapproval, not unmixed with abuse, of the self-interested or blindly ignorant few ?

I continued my work, with the firm conviction that what I did was of no little public value.

At the same time I continued my investigations, with the hope that I might yet find just one grain of wheat amongst the chaff. That one grain, however, has ever eluded me. I have come across wilful impositions in various shapes, and a goodly crop of illusions honestly conceived but altogether lacking the corroboration or logical analysis that make for certainty. And my investigations have taken me the world over.

Of them I shall speak as I go along, relating as briefly as possible the incidents which seem to me to call for particular attention and reasons for the well-considered conclusions I have arrived at.

I would say here that up till some twelve months ago I had ceased to take any further active interest in the subject, which had apparently lost its hold upon the imagination of the credulous public.

But, as an outcome of the Great War, there has, I am grieved to say, come a revival of the craze in its most pernicious and soulless form.

To many who have husbands, sons, brothers, or near male relatives out at the Front, daily and hourly facing danger and death, there has come a natural longing to know something of their welfare ; and when death has snatched them from them, the desire to be put in touch with them in spirit form has become only too insistent.

Some of these sign-seekers, as a result of their longings and expectancies, have had what they assumed to be a first sign direct, which has sent them to a medium—professional or otherwise— for further signs and communications, which these mediums—mostly for a mundane monetary consideration—have not failed to supply.

Seeing the mental risks which these sign-seekers ran, and the rich harvest a number of questionable practitioners were making out of the sorrows and pious longings of their clients, I was moved to issue public warnings on the growth and danger of the craze.

The following, from an article of mine in the *Daily Mail* of 5th January 1917, clearly expresses my views on the subject.   I have the satisfaction of knowing that since then the law has stepped in, and that certain of the more flagrant of the practising mediums have been laid by the heels, and that credulous folk may expect reasonable police assistance against a very heartless and harmful form of imposture :—

" In this advanced, enlightened twentieth century it does indeed seem wonderful that the old-time spiritism, with its unsound pretensions and palpable little tricks, all of which the hard-headed had come to accept as things of the past, should flourish so strongly in our midst.

" But the hankering after the occult, the desire to lift the veil and peep into the future, has ever been with us and never really dies.

" With some it is an honest, deep belief, amounting almost to a religion ; with others, just a pose or a mere money-making game.   It is this deep conviction of the true believer which has given tone to the movement and, at the same time, made possible much of the chicanery attached to it.

" No argument will convince the out-and-out believer that this or that manifestation alleged to have occurred in his presence or through his own mediumship is merely the outcome of expectation or false deductions. With him the difference between facts and inference from facts has no actual existence, and as he has convinced himself of the genuineness of the manifestations which he alleges have been personally vouchsafed him, he declines to see trickery in other directions, and resents as an attack on his own genuineness of belief the unmasking of other people's trickery. In my endeavours to arrive at the truth in connection with so-called 'spirit manifestations' I have, it goes without saying, incurred the condemnation of those worthy folk whose aims and convictions have my profound respect instead of receiving their approval in weeding the cause of its palpable impostures.

. . . . . .

" In a word, I have never yet in any land or with any medium or adept discovered any alleged occult manifestation that was not explicable upon a perfectly natural basis, and which in the majority of instances could not be humanly duplicated under precisely similar conditions. This, as the true believer would say, has been my misfortune. But there it is. So inherent is this hankering after the supernatural in human nature that many would much rather seek for a supernatural than a natural explanation of what may seem mysterious or out of the way to them.

" It is just this longing in human nature upon

2

which these professional psychic frauds are prey-
ing to-day.

" To-day, with its heavy death toll and fateful
uncertainty so closely affecting every section of the
community, is indeed the moment for the practitioners on the shady side of spiritism.   There is
a natural desire among the bereaved, or those in
doubt as to the actual facts surrounding the 'missing,' to seek for news and guidance unobtainable
through the ordinary channels.   These credulous
folk are told that this or that medium is a real
wonder who has given such and such person the
most astounding revelations.   So what has been
vouchsafed others can quite as well be revealed to
them.   Hence the run upon the plausible 'crooks,'
who so readily trade upon their credulity.

"The foolish, credulous dupes never for a moment
consider the utter incongruousness of the association of their beloved dead or missing with these
professional ' spookists.'   It never enters their
heads that if the spirit of anyone dear to them
could return at all, it would be to them direct that
his return would be manifested, and that to have
to go to some strange ' crook ' and part with
money for the privilege of being put in touch with
the spirit is the height of absurdity.   They are
told that they themselves are not *mediumistic*, and
that it is only through the truly *mediumistic* are
such communications possible.   Besides, it is the
fashion or ' the thing ' to go to these mediums,
who, ' poor dears,' must live and who are entitled
to payment for the exhaustion they frequently
undergo in getting in touch with the spirits.   No

labourer, in fact, is so worthy of his hire as one in the spiritual vineyard.

" And the wine he presses as he rakes in the notes is the flow of tears from the sorrowful and distressed.

" It is not only a shady business, but it is a mean and cruel one, and should be put an end to. If the foolish cannot or will not protect themselves, they must be protected against their own folly.

.   .   .   .   .   .

" General Smith-Dorrien's crusade against vice had for its object the well-being of the young soldier ; but the vice, in all its alluring naturalness of which he complains, is, to put it quite bluntly, mild in its injurious effects as compared with the possibilities of harm arising to these soldiers' sorrowing relatives in their pursuit of the unnatural. Any mental authority will testify to the mental dangers associated with such practices.

" There is not space for me here in which to relate my impressions and experiences of spirits I have known, together with other phases of the so-called occult. It forms too long a story. I would, however, like to say that I am desirous of extending my knowledge of spiritism and occultism so as to include the latest exponents of the mystic art. I am quite open to conviction, and should rejoice to find something which, under proper test conditions and with due investigation, proved itself beyond question the outcome of spirit power. A manifestation which is capable of being demonstrated can alone be beyond question when done under conditions from which all chances of trickery are eliminated.   There are apparently other forms of 'spirit power' which, while not depending upon outward and visible demonstrations for their proof, claim to give the inquirer glimpses into the past, present, and future.   They, too, clipped of their patter and ungraspable ambiguousness, are interesting in their way as showing on what lines certain spirits alone can or will work.

" Honestly, the whole of my inquiring, investigating soul goes out to all : the bootless materialised form in white, the three dead friends on the slips of paper, the passing of matter through matter, the sepulchral voice that comes from the Beyond finally to find escape through the medium's own mouth, the clutching spirit-controlled hand that scribbles endless messages from the other world regardless of the shortage of paper in this.   Yes, I am ready and eager to become closely acquainted with them all, and to make known to the world the truth that in them is."

To the opinions expressed above I have nothing to add.   I am still seeking for proofs, still anxious to be convinced.   To my request for enlightenment I received upwards of one hundred letters ; but although I was again and again assured that such and such a thing had undoubtedly occurred, there was no corroborative evidence of its occurrence and no willingness to have the manifestation repeated under proper test conditions.   This inability to guarantee a repetition of an occurrence which has caused bewilderment or intense personal satisfaction, according to belief or temperament, is understandable from the fact that such visitation has in all probability nothing more behind it than is contained in the mere mind's-eye form of proof.

But in these purely subjective, as distinct from objective, occurrences certain men prominent in Literature and Science profess to see a proof of a life Beyond, and of the ability of that spirit life to make itself seen, known and understood. In support of this contention not an atom of actual proof is advanced ; and it simply serves to give a wholly unnecessary fillip to a movement which might, to the moral and mental well-being of those who are disposed to follow it, be left severely alone.

The harm that may be worked amongst such followers, too ill-equipped mentally to correctly diagnose and appraise the real value of the phenomena associated therewith, causes me to place my experiences and conclusions in the present form before the public.

CHAPTER II

MONARCHS AND MYSTICS

THE hankering after the uncanny, the dabbling in the so-called occult, is by no means confined to emotional women and mentally ill-balanced men with more time on their hands than they know what to do with, and more inner longings than they know well how to check or control.

Their beliefs, if they do not bring them a salutary disillusion, end generally in dissatisfaction or disappointment. That is their own affair. But it is quite another thing when the mystic art casts its spell over a country's rulers, influencing their interior and exterior policies, to the general injury and danger.

It is beyond question that mystic influence had not a little to do with the downfall of the Romanoffs and the great upheaval in Russia. The dabbling in the supernatural at the Russian Court is by no means a new thing. It dates back years. It came in with the visit of D. D. Home, and went out with the removal of the unspeakable Rasputin.

Home succeeded in capturing the society of more than one European capital ; but I fancy he did best in Petrograd. He finally managed to

impress a Russian princess, a goddaughter of the
Tzar Alexander II., to the extent of getting her
to give him her hand and fortune.

His social success here in London was not
inconsiderable.

Home gave a tone to Modern Spiritism, and—
to use an Americanism—was looked upon by the
faithful as quite a "tony" medium.   His bag of
spiritual tricks included materialisation and dematerialisation ; but his chief card was "levita-
tion."   There were two noble lords who, in their
mind's eye at least, saw him float in and out of an
open window in a west-end London house, and duly
testified to the fact.   Nothing, I believe, would
convince them of the fallacy of the pretension.
In these days of the conquest of the air, how
useful the floating art might have been made,
especially if Home, as claimed, could make himself invulnerable !

Whilst in Petrograd—so at least a famous
diplomat assured me when I was there—Home
did a feat of dematerialisation before the Court
which, had it not been for the favour in which
he was held in high places, might have curtailed
his liberty for a period.

He had demateralised a splendid row of emeralds
lent the "dear spirits" for the purpose of the
test ; but up to the time of his departure from
the séance, the emeralds, for some occult reason,
had declined to materialise and thus be handed
back to the confiding owner.   They were, of
course, in spirit land engaging the attention of
the spooks, who seem to have a pretty taste for

valuable jewels. But the chief of the police had not that faith in spiritual probity generally accepted at the Court, and, before leaving the palace, Home was searched, and—so the story came to me—the dematerialised emeralds were found materialising in his coat-tail pocket. They had been placed there by an evil spirit, of course. But the police chief impressed upon the medium that the climate of the Russian capital might not be good for his health—that an early departure would probably benefit it. Home took the hint and his early departure. To his dying day, I think, he regretted the interference of the evil spirit. It would have been so much more satisfactory for the jewels to have remained dematerialising in spirit land, to be materialised at will with no interfering police around, for they were of great earthly value.

History has an odd habit of repeating itself even in connection with spiritualistic affairs.

During the crisis associated with the approaching abdication of the Tzar Nicholas, it was impossible to get in touch with ministers who counted, on account of their being engrossed in a spiritualistic séance. How ill the controlling spirits at this séance advised the sitters, and failed to get in proper celestial touch with the to-be-dethroned monarch, events have shown.

During my first visit to Petrograd there was another crisis in the air, which, if it had come to a head, would have had very far-reaching effects. To my great surprise I found that hardened diplomatic old sinner, Count Peter Shuvalow, sitting with a number of high ministers of state at a round table consulting the " dear spirits " as to what could happen, and so forth. His Excellency affected to be surprised at my disbelief in the powers of the spirits to manifest in the manner anticipated by the sitters. But, all the same, I was distinctly of the private opinion that at heart his belief in the reality of such phenomena did not exceed my own. He was, I conjectured, but playing a game, just because it was at the moment diplomatic to so play it.

Whilst ambassador in London he played the game of make-believe to an extent never yet approached by the diplomatic representative of any other country attached to the Court of St James. Well I remember Mr Henry Labouchere impressing upon me, on the eve of my departure for Russia, the wisdom of studying closely the ex-Ambassador, who, shortly after his return to Petrograd, had been appointed head of the dreaded Third Section.

" As a subject," added Labby, " you will find him the hardest nut you have ever tried to crack. To judge him by appearances, or to accept any statement as indicative of his actual thoughts, is to make the greatest mistake possible. I have in mind the critical days of the Russo-Turkish war, when the goody-goodies of Society thought how deplorable it was that so gifted a man, holding so distinguished a position, should drink so heavily and take so little trouble to hide the fact from those with whom, in accordance with his position, he associated. But it was all a game ; and, I must confess, he played it remarkably cleverly. It enabled him to eavesdrop without being suspected, and to let out grave secrets whilst seemingly in his cups, which, instead of being an act of grave indiscretion, was just a part of his little game.   I always had my suspicion that he painted his nose at times in order to more completely look the part."

Labby, from his at one time connection with the British Embassy in Petrograd, knew the Russian diplomatic world pretty well ; but his knowledge of Russian diplomats did not, I fancy, include General Ignatieff, the author of the famous San Stefano Treaty.   I had ample opportunities of studying both him and Peter Shuvalow ; and in the matter of mental deception and verbal unmeaningness the ex-head of the dreaded Third Section was a guileless child as compared with the treaty-drawer.

Count Paul Shuvalow, Peter's brother, whom I saw frequently in Petrograd, and subsequently in Berlin, where he was the Tzar's ambassador, leaving there to succeed General Gourko as Governor-General of Poland, had not only a real belief in the occult, but was convinced that he himself was genuinely psychic.   In diplomatic circles in Berlin it was generally assumed that his Excellency was not quite all there.   But his seeming absent-mindedness and funny little ways were too, I am sure, just a part of his own game.

Rasputin would never have flourished or have exercised the slightest Court influence had he been up against Paul Shuvalow.   Had it been necessary, in order to have effectively combated that unspeakable person's evil influence, he would, I have no doubt, have boldly declared himself a medium controlled by celestial beings of the highest probity, who not only denied Rasputin's alleged powers, but most strongly condemned his habits and practices.   Count Paul was a gentleman as well as an astute man of the world.   He knew by instinct the right card to play in mysticism as well as in diplomacy, according to the audience he sought to impress.

Tzar Alexander III. had no great faith, if any at all, in mystic phenomena ; but at times he had moods of religious mysticism.   In those moods he would retire within his own shell, as it were, and be more or less unapproachable by anyone. Spiritualistic practices had to cry a halt at the Russian Court during his reign.

But the Tzar Nicholas II. was a man of a different mental and physical fibre from that of his father.   From an early period he had a leaning towards mysticism, and in the end mysticism got the upper hand, which is its way with weak natures, whether they wear a crown or the orthodox headgear of middle-class respectability.

The ex-Tzaritsa had this leaning too ; but it arose, I fancy, more from the exactions of her position than from any inner promptings.   I have always had the impression that, had she been born in the Middle Ages instead of the prosaic nineteenth century, the Tzaritsa, by temperament and instinct and sincere religious convictions, would have made a really first-class saint.

I never forgot the impression she made upon me at our first meeting. It was at Darmstadt ; and I had the honour of being presented to her by her father. She was then quite young, very spirituelle, and seemingly most ingenuous. I had but recently returned from Russia, where, I gathered, my work had been followed with interest at the Hesse-Darmstadt Grand Ducal Court.

Said the Princess to me—and I use her words, of which I took a firm mental note, reciting them again and again during the years that followed— " Now, you have been to Russia, and have, I hear, met and read everybody. Do tell me quite frankly what is your real opinion of the country and its people ? "

I told her, with but few reservations.

" I thank you very much," she replied. " I did so much want to know your real and honest opinion ; and you have had such a striking experience."

" You know," she added, as I was bowing my farewell, " that Russia is a country I never really wish to go to. My sister is, I think, one of the most unhappy women in the world."

This was long before the assassin removed the husband of her sister, the Grand Duke Serge, from a world which he had so constantly outraged. He indeed was a coarse, evil degenerate.

With her betrothal to the heir to the Russian throne, fate destroyed the girlish hopes of Queen Victoria's grand-daughter.

I am strongly of opinion that, in becoming betrothed to the Tzarevitch, she was just as much a necessary victim to policy as was Brieux's Egyptian Maiden, thrown to the crocodiles so that, the gods being appeased, the Nile would rise. Faith—blind, unquestioning faith—influenced the Egyptian. Duty—unquestioning Duty—influenced the German Princess. At the moment Duty called for what she considered the sacrifice ; her heart, one may take it, was no more in the making of a home in Russia than it was that night she laid bare her thoughts to me on the subject in Darmstadt.

The sense of Duty, stern, relentless Duty, went with her to Petrograd, surrounded her, absorbed her, obsessed her. In her heart, no doubt, she asked why Fate had called upon her rather than upon anyone else to make the requisite sacrifice. At the same time she buoyed herself up with the assurance that she was but obeying Duty's demands, and the deeply religious strain within her took some comfort in the fact that the ways of Providence are inscrutable, and that it is not for mortals to reason the why or wherefore of Providence's decrees. But that germ of mystic instinct—more of a religious foundation than anything else—that was early inborn in her grew and grew, until the inclination came to take a peep at the Beyond, to discover what Providence really meant by placing her in the position she was occupying. There were not failing those about her who played upon this religious mystic instinct. But recognised ecclesiastics, who came with their consolations, were too orthodox, too commonplace, in fact, to satisfy her cravings for an insight into the unknown. Then came the temptation to see what professed occultists could do. Those around her told her fairy tales of this or that mystic, whose powers were as divinely inspired as his manifestations were astounding. Her Majesty had not the strength to resist the temptation, nor the necessary training to discriminate the false from the true.

This preliminary dabbling in the mystic through the well-remunerated agency of insinuating impostors paved the way for the entrance on the scene of the much-talked-of medium, Philippe. How any sane person could have attributed supernatural powers to a man of his type passes all understanding. He was an unmitigated *poseur*, possessing boundless self-assurance and an elementary knowledge of sleight-of-hand. He affected silk stockings, silver-buckled shoes, and velvet shorts. Another impression he conveyed to me was, that any spirits he might control would have their spiritual home in some Montmartre cabaret, rather than in the celestial regions from which they are supposed to be drawn. But Philippe came from Paris to Petrograd not only with a reputation as a mystic, but as one who, whilst being a darling of the gods, was at the same time the darling of his fair devotees in the French capital.

It made one sick when news reached one of the tremendous fuss that was made over this oily fraud, and I was for going hot haste to Russia to expose the impostor, as I had some years before caused the bringing to book of the medium Bastian, when he was in Vienna trying to rope in the Crown

Prince Rudolph. I had previously exposed this same medium masquerading as a spirit at a séance in London, and I knew it went without saying that the spirit forms he could produce in the Viennese capital could not be any more the real thing than the one I laid by the heels here. Of this worthy and his manifestations I have something to say in the next chapter.

Philippe, according to accounts which reached me, reaped quite a golden harvest whilst in the Russian capital. And the bounder, at one time, was thankful for any small loose change when he had " demonstrated " before me.

His reputation as a lady-killer, which he brought with him from Paris, stood him in good stead with the highly placed fair sex in Petrograd. It was discovered that he was not only very fascinating, but there was something about his appearance which was quite apostolic. Fancy an apostle in velvet knee-breeches and silver-buckled shoes, and with an up-to-date boulevardier leer !

But the apostolic card was a good one to play. How he must have inwardly blessed the fatuous female who made the discovery ! It was the means of bringing him into close mystic, spiritual touch with the Tzaritsa. From impressing her and her entourage with his mystic gifts, which, truth to tell, were, as demonstrated, of no high order and of but little originality, Philippe gradually assumed the rôle of a prophet. It was one he particularly fancied himself in, and one which his women admirers who had discovered the apostolic look thought became him perfectly.

At that time the Tzaritsa was hungering for prophecy; and who so likely to successfully gratify her as this gifted being in such close touch with the spiritual world?

It is only those closely associated with her Majesty at that period who knew how near to her heart was the wish to have a son, and how she sought for spiritual confirmation of her hopes.

Philippe, it goes without saying, turned his prophetic utterances in the direction desired. Her Majesty would assuredly give birth to a son. So it was written, and so it would be—at her next accouchement. But it happened to be a girl on that occasion. Nothing daunted, Philippe had another try; but, alas for his reputation as a prophet, there was another girl.

The failures of Philippe in the prophetic line made room for Rasputin, a far more sinister and dangerous impostor than the one he supplanted.

Rasputin was brought into touch with the Tzaritsa through her sister, the Grand Duchess Serge, who since the assassination of her disreputable husband had more or less retired from the affairs of the world and had embraced religion with both arms, as it were, by way of consolation.

I have already said how the Tzaritsa as a girl had expressed her belief in her sister being the unhappiest woman in the world. A year ago a very distinguished lady journalist and traveller, who came to interview me as a psychologist for a great American newspaper combination, and to whom I related this fact, replied, "I have seen the

Grand Duchess since you have—quite recently, in fact.   Unhappy ?   That to-day falls far short of my reading of her.   She is the most tragic figure, I think, I have ever seen."

And her introduction to Rasputin was the first step in the tragedy that was to follow.

The tragic Grand Duchess caught at any straw that floated in the murky atmosphere of her religious obsession.   She saw in Rasputin a golden bridge on which she could walk with certainty of getting into close touch with the unknown.   This religious obsession blinded her to the creature's manifest ignorance and unmitigated commonality. He was the one who, being in such direct communion with the other world, would be able to give the true prophetic utterance her distressed sister was so much in need of.

Rasputin was a loathsome person, but, with women, there was about him a certain hypnotic force that exercised a peculiar sway.   Men, who did not feel this hypnotic force, utterly failed to understand his influence ; but he worked through the women, and they smoothed down the opposition amongst the men.   A photo I had shown me, taken but a few weeks before his " removal," showed Rasputin seated with a number of women followers grouped about him.   The lecherous look on most of these women's faces was disgusting, and the dreamy, hypnotised appearance of others altogether pitiful.

His rôle when at Court was not so much to work miracles after the fashion of Philippe and other mystics who had preceded him, but to pose as one especially endowed with grace, a sort of holy man thrown amongst humans for their moral exaltation and spiritual advancement. The Tzaritsa was in the mood to be taken in ; and taken in by him she assuredly was. The pity of it ! And when his prophecy came off about the birth of a son, succeeding at the first shot where Philippe had twice gone wrong, her faith in the impostor became unshakable.

Many stories have from time to time reached me about the man's libertinage, and the grave danger he had become to many a highly placed household ; but his amorous adventures—beyond the fact that they afforded me one more proof how soft morally women can become when they mentally succumb to mediumistic imposture—did not particularly interest me. I must, however, confess to some personal satisfaction over his dramatic removal from this earthly sphere, coupling with it the regret that it had not taken place long before.

Could the Tzaritsa's eyes have been opened to the true character of the man ? Maybe, if one had been on the spot and had practically demonstrated the hollowness of his pretensions, or if the Tzar Nicholas had been a stronger man with the mental astuteness and strength to see the falsity of the rascal's claims, and the physical determination to put his foot down and summarily banish him from the Court. But, instead of rejoicing at the impostor's removal, the Tzar, I am given to understand, strongly resented the steps that had been taken, and the actors in the tragedy came within his severe personal displeasure.

As it was, an ignorant and depraved mystic, who was said to have been in German pay, was certainly indirectly, if not actually directly, the means of ending the Romanoff dynasty. Shade of the Great Peter !

.   .   .   .   .   .

But while the Romanoff dynasty has ceased to exist, it is not the only European dynasty that has been severely shaken through association with mystic adventurers.

During the reign of the late King of Würtemberg an American spirit medium exercised an extraordinary influence over that monarch's mind. He became a great power in the land, and gravely interfered with the nation's internal affairs. He was, indeed, so much the power behind the throne that plots were made by the disgruntled loyalists to abduct him or to remove him by means that permit of no return journey. But, despite the intense disgust the King's favouritism towards his unworthy protégé caused amongst his people of all ranks, his Majesty refused to cast him off, and declared his firm belief in the man's claims to supernatural powers.

And he was but an ordinary medium after all, with just a full bag of commonplace mediumistic fakes. The King in his patronage of his pet seer went from blunder to blunder, the culminating act being his appointment as a Councillor of State, with the title of Count. With this one of two things had to happen. Either the King or the Count had to go ; upon this all that was influential in the kingdom of Würtemberg was determined.

It ended in the King remaining and the Count leaving, with, I understand, the patent of nobility and as much wealth as he could collect in the brief period allowed him for collection.

What has finally become of this astute Yankee medium I do not know. When he left Germany he returned as quickly as possible to the land of his birth, there to relate to a rigid democracy what blithering idiots some monarchs can be. Out of his Würtemberg spoils, I have, however, heard, he acquired a ranch somewhere out West.

Amongst the European Courts to which I had the honour of being invited was that of Würtemberg ; and, in another work, I have related how good a " subject " I found the present King, who, by the by, has none of those little crankisms which distinguished his predecessor of spiritualistic proclivities. Between moments of puffing at and partly chewing the end of a most unattractive-looking black cigar, his Majesty interjected some exceedingly strong but certainly common-sense ideas as to the rascality of professed mystics and the incalculable folly of their dupes. He was seemingly much interested in my views of the mystic art, and my expositions of some of the phenomena for which supernatural agency had been claimed.

" This mystic business is a lot of d—— nonsense," he concluded ; with which conclusion I was in full agreement.

. . . . .

Napoleon III. was mystically inclined, and in the first instance was disposed to look upon

Home as a celestially endowed being far above the common.

But the medium put his foot in it, and, at the same time, himself out of Court, when he undertook to " materialise " Napoleon I. The form of the Great Napoleon was duly " materialised " —in the dark—at the séance which the then Emperor of the French attended.

The Emperor—so the story has come down to me—was anxious for physical proof of the form's presence. A grip of the hand, a friendly pat on the shoulder, a kiss of kinship, anything to prove that the form claimed to be hovering near, was substantial in its materialisation, and not a mere shadowy, optical illusion.

The proof came, but not in the way his Majesty either expected or desired.

In rising, better to greet the spirit form—so the story continues—he felt himself kicked in the darkness—yes, he, the Destiny of France, actually kicked from behind, and with no light foot either, and in a place which prevented him from sitting down in comfort for the rest of the evening.

Needless to say, the Emperor did not seek a repetition of his great relative's materialisation ; and he had no further use for Home or his alleged mediumistic gifts. But for that *mal à propos* kick, Home, cementing his influence at the Court, might have shaped the Emperor's policy better than he himself shaped it. Who can say ? That is just one of those might-have-beens to which subsequent events can provide no conclusive reply. From France Home went to Italy, and shortly after he himself became a spirit, but I have not heard of his spirit form materialising at a séance for the delectation of his admirers and followers whilst in the flesh.

Home was before my time, so I can speak of his mystic wonders only at second hand. How, by the by, Home's flying art would have interested Lord Northcliffe, and what a big fat cheque would have been his if he could have afforded material proof of his art of conquering the air to that enterprising nobleman's satisfaction !

.   .   .   .   .   .

The Sultan Abdul Hamid was himself of a distinctly mystic temperament ; and he had an inborn hankering after the mystical. His fancy, however, did not run much in the direction of Western magic or its exponents. But within my personal knowledge his Majesty made one striking exception. The seer was a German, and he came to Constantinople claiming to be " the world's greatest magician." German intrigue was rampant on the banks of the Bosphorus at that time ; and the magician was taken up by the German Embassy for purposes best known to his Excellency the Ambassador and his inner ring of officials. A séance was procured for him at Yildiz Kiosk, for the modest fee of one thousand pounds, Turkish. He was, as skilled "magicians" go, a poor exponent of the magic art ; but his thin little sleight-of-hand tricks found favour with the gloomy, jerky-minded potentate. It was, I afterwards discovered, a part of the Ambassador's little plan that this made-in-Germany specimen of the magic art should not appear to be too deep or skilful. It was enough for him to demonstrate what his Majesty could easily follow and discuss. To have bewildered the Sultan or given him cause for serious reflection would have collided with the German policy then being worked. For the Sultan's favourite soothsayer had impressed upon his Majesty the possible advent of a "wise man" from the West, who, according to tradition, was to greatly menace the safety of the reigning Padishah and be the signal of the ultimate overthrow of the Ottoman Empire. That this wise man could possibly be of German origin was of course unthinkable.

The chief Dragoman of the British Embassy duly acquainted my Ambassador, with whom I had had a somewhat close personal acquaintance extending over a period of years, of this tradition with which the Sultan was obsessed, and added that it was generally accepted in Court circles that I and no other was the veritable incarnation of the prophecy. This afforded his Excellency, personally, considerable amusement ; but at the same time he cautioned me not to take the matter too lightly.

" Be most careful in what you say or in what you do, for every room here, no matter how hermetically closed, has both eyes and ears," was his seriously meant advice.

At a little dinner at the Embassy, at which the German Ambassador and other members of the Corps Diplomatique were present, the subject turned on mystics and mysticism, and the " wise

man" tradition. Said my Ambassador jokingly,
"So, it appears that this terrible wise man is
British after all, and the mantle of the prophecy
has fallen on our young friend's shoulders," indicating me and looking, as I thought at the time,
somewhat pointedly at Germany's diplomatic
representative. "Well," he went on, "I have
known him for some years, and this is the first
time I am expected to view him in the light
of a wise man."

"No, sir," I replied, "anyone more foolish or
powerless does not exist in all Pera."

There was an all-round laugh, and the subject
dropped.

The Introducer of the Corps Diplomatique,
with whom I had some acquaintance, was a man
with considerable knowledge of the working of
the inner circle at Yildiz Kiosk. Outwardly he
was one of the most charming men attached to the
Court, and he went by the sobriquet of "Sugar
Pasha." Oh! that sweet smile of his, when,
one evening, at a little festivity at his palace, I,
in the course of an opportune aside, asked him
what I had done to be designated the wise man
of the prophecy.

"You? my young friend, you? Impossible!"
and he waved away the thought with a gesture
that was most becoming, if not altogether convincing. "No, my dear friend, some evil-minded
person has spread this report just to annoy you.
His Majesty, I happen to know, thinks highly
of your art, and has set you down for personal
distinction."

How beautifully Sugar Pasha could lie !

At my public meeting my attention, by some one in the know, was drawn to the fact that the hall contained a large number of the Sultan's most trusted secret agents, some of them being hidden under the seats of the gallery at the back, taking furtive notes of everything I said and did; in such personal esteem did his Majesty hold me.

Amongst my acquaintances at Constantinople was a certain Bey who, through his position, was in closer touch with the Sultan than any other official I knew. So far as it is given a Westerner to directly understand the true workings of the Oriental mind, I had arrived at the conclusion that the said Bey was not unfriendly disposed towards me, and that, so far as his training and mental reservation would permit, he could be fairly frank with me. Amongst other European languages he spoke English excellently, and to be able to converse with him direct in one's mother tongue was certainly an advantage. The Bey's functions at Yildiz Kiosk were to communicate to his master on their arrival at any time in the night the contents of all special cables and telegrams that might arrive there. The Sultan's personal telegraphic correspondence was both extensive and peculiar. In this way the Bey came into very close touch with his august master and saw him in his varying moods and mental twistings as few others saw him.

To him I repaired one evening, the day following a Selamlik at which I had been present and where I had had a highly interesting though obviously brief conversation with Von der Goltz Pasha, whose opinion, by the by, of Abdul Hamid was not exactly flattering. He had no patience with the Sultan's almost puerile superstitions, and his lack of mental straightforwardness and both physical and moral courage were not appealing factors to this eminent soldier, who, I believe, had suffered from his Majesty's vacillating policy.

I had to wait some time before I could be received by the Bey, and I did the waiting in a long passage, up and down which people seemingly of little or no importance constantly flitted. At last I got into the Bey's presence. He was quite alone, although I had been assured he was neckdeep in engagements.

Said he in a low voice, as the door closed upon my entrance, " Did you notice anyone particular outside ? "

" No, only your brother," I replied.

" And he is the most dangerous of the lot." His voice was a mere whisper by this time.

" Come in here," he added, offering me a cigarette. Being Ramazan, and many hours from sunset, he did not himself smoke.

We passed into an adjoining room which happened to be his bedroom. He quickly closed the door, tried the handle of the door opening on to the passage, gave a hurried glance round the room, then stooped and looked under the bed.

" Afraid of ghosts ? " I asked, with some curiosity in my voice.

" Sh ! " and his finger went to his lips.

"Ghosts, no.   They can't hurt ; it's the living who can.   One never knows who may be listening."

" But the coast seems pretty clear now."

" Yes !   I think we can talk now," but as he said it he gave another quick, furtive look around the room.   " And in what way can my poor services be of use to you ?   They, as you know, are entirely at your disposal."

I bowed my acknowledgments, and then, as deftly as I could, brought up the subject of that, to me, thread-worn prophecy concerning the wise man from the West.   The Bey shrugged his shoulders almost pityingly.

" But you, whose vocation it is to combat superstitions, put no faith in prophecies ? "

" Prophets as a rule," I replied, " are more human in their errors than ordinary mortals. But the prophet responsible for this particular prophecy would appear to have had being untold years before my existence could ever have been thought of."

" You ! surely no one associates you with the prophecy ? "   His kindly, sympathetic look which accompanied the words was most touching.

" You ! of course not ; you are an enlightened man, and stupidity of this kind does not go with enlightenment.   But, leaving me out of the question, you, I suppose, like the rest, believe there may be something after all in the prophecy ?

" And you, who read minds as an open book, ask me what I think, what I believe ? "   This with a gentle reproving air, tendered with obvious flattery.

" Well, then, I read that you are not without a certain amount of belief."

" And at the same time you read, it is not always well and wise to let the tongue give expression to the thought."

" That at least is frank."

" My friend, whenever was I not perfectly frank with you? And never was I more so than now."

Which perfect frankness, to use an Americanism, did not cut much ice with me.

And as to the careful watchfulness of official "observers" at my public meeting? That, I knew, was a matter that would come well within the Bey's knowledge, and in a way indirectly associated with his personal supervision.

Oh! that little matter. Again came out that old tag. It was just like his Majesty's close interest in me and my work. Having this deep interest, he, obviously, was anxious to have a full and correct report of what I did, and how I did it, from the public as distinct from the private point of view. And who so well able to furnish this report as trained, trusted observers whose observations and reports could be relied upon?

" What, my friend, we have to guard against in this world is the lying and underworking of our enemies. How I have suffered from it!"

The look which followed these words was that of a martyr.

" And you, my friend, are, I fear, a victim of the same evildoers, but they will be confounded, and upon my friendship you can rely." Out went his hand, and his face beamed friendly regard of the highest order.

" My little affair is of too little moment to occupy your attention. But, Bey, can it by a stretch of imagination be associated with something political? The ways of political purpose are often devious, and, to the unwary, are full of pitfalls."

" Politics? They are no concern of mine. The laughing whisper of a pretty woman is of far more interest to me than the gravest utterance of the most distinguished diplomat."

" And yet every message which comes over the wires bringing requests or answers that may affect the political affairs of kingdoms come first into your hands."

" True, but I see nothing with my own eyes. I am but a conduit pipe, and blind as a bat whilst making the conveyance. And again, I have a shocking memory. The tongue cannot repeat what the mind does not remember. My enemies, who work ceaselessly for my undoing, may say otherwise ; but truth always prevails in the end."

He was in that moment the embodiment of Truth.

I was not to see my friend the Bey again, as shortly after I took the boat to Varna, on my way to obtain a closer acquaintance with the Balkan peoples and their rulers.

Whether the " Wise Man from the West" stunt had a real place in prophecy or whether it had origin in the inner consciousness of the Sultan's pet soothsayer, I am unable to say with any definiteness. As put to him, Abdul Hamid, I fancy, believed it to the letter. His was a mind that was steeped in superstition, and the mystic vapourings of his soothsayers had without doubt considerable influence with him.

I fancy I was picked out as the wise man of the alleged prophecy on account of an incident that had happened a short time before in Cairo. A Prince of the Druses had by special request taken me to see a very learned Sheikh, whose word, as a sort of holy man, had great weight in the Mahommedan world.

The Sheikh expressed curiosity as to my powers of reading thoughts, but his curiosity was, I could see, heavily fringed with suspicion and hostility. But I made the attempt at reading his thought. He was not a good subject. This, considering his mental attitude at the start, did not surprise me. I had previously successfully experimented with the Druse Prince, which success apparently neither interested nor surprised the Sheikh. It was his own thoughts he wished to have read.

The test with him consisted in finding something he had previously hidden in another room to the one in which we were assembled. I took the Sheikh and roamed with him about that gloomy old palace of the first Abbas, without getting any indication as to the place on which his thoughts were supposed to be concentrated. He seemingly thought of everything and everywhere but the particular locality. As a matter of fact, his mental antagonism gave me the very clue

he was anxious not to disclose. We had arrived
in a room in which was a table, and upon it was
lying a fairly massive book. I could feel that
that book was in his thoughts, but that he did not
wish me to go to it. Indeed, he almost dragged me
from it from time to time. This was my indication. I placed my hand upon the book and quickly
threw it open. Between the leaves—indeed,
piercing a particular verse—was the object, a pin
previously taken from his own garment. The face
of the Sheikh at that moment was indeed an interesting study. Perplexity and anger were clearly
outlined thereon. I put the perplexity down to
his doubts as to my ability to read his thoughts,
and the angry end of it to my having succeeded.

But I afterwards knew that the book in question
was the Koran, and that the pin had been stuck
in a passage containing an injunction against magic
and evil-doers.

Now, my success should have proved beyond
doubt that the passage did not apply to me. But
this conclusion was not accepted by the Sheikh,
who was supposed to be a really great logician.
Apart from his own mental attitude towards me,
he thought the precaution that, according to his
religious belief, he had taken would in itself have
negatived the possibility of a successful issue to
the test.

An account of the experiment, which seemed
to my friends to have exceptional interest, was sent
to the vernacular press in Constantinople, but the
order went forth that nothing on the subject was
to be printed, and not even the *Levant Herald*,

so the editor courteously informed me, could mention it in English.

Now, one can understand how the lip-serving soothsayer, having started the hare of prophecy, turned, as it were, the hunt upon me. I was fair game because I was British. The Sultan undoubtedly believed in the prophecy, and in his fear-racked way was dreading the falling shadow of the coming Wise Man from the West.

All this happened but a comparatively short time before the visit of the German Kaiser with his fantastic dreams of Eastern Empire, which I dealt with in a somewhat lengthy article at an early stage of the present war.

The German diplomatists and their agents were busily doing the spade-work preparatory to this visit. They spent money lavishly and lied without stint. The Kaiser on his arrival was highly gratified at the success of the pro-German propaganda. I think I may be permitted to say that those in the inner diplomatic ring, such, for instance, as M. Paul Cambon, who then represented the interests of France at the Sublime Porte, as he to-day so ably represents them here at the Court of St James, and that brilliant diplomat, Sir Arthur Nicolson, then attached to the British Embassy, were well aware of the subtle activity of this propaganda, and one may take it they acted accordingly.

Sir Arthur understood German psychology as well as the German on his part failed to understand that of Sir Arthur; and the official German dislike of the British diplomat who has done so

much to upset Germanic plans is not surprising.
On his retirement from the Permanent Under-
Secretaryship of the Foreign Office the inspired
Berlin Press gleefully shouted with one voice,
" There goes the bitterest and most prejudiced
foe Germany has ever had."

To return to the " wise man " business. Shortly
after I had left Constantinople, an event happened
which terribly jarred upon poor Abdul's nerves.
A bridge over which he was passing on his way to
a special service at the mosque collapsed. Whilst
he himself got safely over, several lives were lost,
and it was generally considered that the Sultan
had had a lucky escape.

I was in Bucharest at the time, and, obviously,
although I had no more connection with the
event than the man in the moon, I was sincerely
congratulated by more than one person on the
fact of my being absent from the Turkish capital
at the time.

Personal observation and experience cause me
to pin very little faith on so-called prophetic utterances. There is to my mind far too much of the
after-the-event atmosphere about them, as a rule,
to carry conviction.

But, frankly, I am inclined to place more credence on that particular Turkish prophecy than
any that has been brought to my attention.

Events subsequent to its having come first
within my knowledge seem distinctly to point
to the coming of a man from the West who was
to work the undoing of Abdul and the downfall
of the Turkish Empire. That man was the

4

Kaiser. His coming brought bad luck to the Sultan. He lost his throne, and the downfall of the Turkish Empire, as Abdul Hamid knew it, is equally certain. If the occult agency through which the seer influencing Abdul Hamid worked had been worth its salt, it would at once have put its finger upon the Kaiser William as the danger-spot. But these occult agencies, these seers, these all-wise interpreters of prophecies never really do anything worth doing, not even when the stability of a despotic monarch and the integrity of a considerable Empire are at stake.[1]

. . . . . .

Whilst, it is true, there are few things indeed one can with justice place to the Kaiser's credit, I do think in perfect fairness he may be credited with the wisdom of not dabbling in common occultism or in being influenced, as some other monarchs have been, by personal mystics and arrant spiritualistic impostors.

But, on the other hand, it must be said, when the Kaiser is there, there is not room for two at the same table, and this, I take it, may apply to a celestial as well as a terrestrial personage.

The Kaiser, in a word, is his own medium. He would scorn working through any other medium, no matter how mystically endowed. By his utter-

[1] Since this was in type, Abdul Hamid has joined his fathers. In Shadeland he possibly may gain a more accurate knowledge of the value of prophecy than was vouchsafed him on earth. In the fullness of time he may be able to compare notes as to their earthly past with William of Hohenzollern, who will, one imagines, be translated to the same plane as that adorned by the ex-Sultan.

ances one can tell how much he is in direct touch with the other world, and the air with which he says it is conviction itself of his personal belief in its reality.

And yet one day even he may be caused to " manifest " at some mean back-room séance through the mediumship of some needy practitioner who sees money in him as a spirit star turn.

Far greater men than the Kaiser, when they have become spirits, have suffered a like indignity at the hands of those professing to be in touch with the other world.

. . . . . .

The Emperor Carl of Austria, whose father, by the by, evinced considerable interest in my work, has, I understand, spiritualistic tendencies. These he has acquired from his mother, who is very superstitious and disposed to consider herself protected by other world influences. She saw in the events leading to the placing of her son on the throne the hand of Fate. I wonder if she has read the hand of Fate as to the future of the Hapsburg dynasty ?

So far the Kaiser Carl has not taken to his bosom a professional occultist to be his guide, philosopher, and friend in the matter of statecraft. In such a matter, Kaiser Wilhelm would certainly have something to say. Whatever guiding there is to be done, his alone must be the brain and the hand to do it—alike in mundane and other-world affairs.

. . . . . .

King Ferdinand of Bulgaria is another monarch who has mystical tendencies. He is a nervous creature, afraid of his own shadow, and has a habit of " seeing ghosts." It is said he is haunted by the shade of Stambuloff, the " Bismarck of the Balkans," whom, it is alleged, he indirectly caused to be done to death. The last time I saw Stambuloff, a little while before his assassination, he had a sort of premonition that his days on earth would not be long. What a difference between the two men—the ruler and the minister ! Stambuloff had a mental grip and force of character that never failed to impress anyone with whom he came in contact. Ferdinand has a shifty mind and about as much strength of character as a jelly-fish. Stambuloff, who, I gathered, did not hold Bulgaria's ruler in any high esteem, was far too dominant a person to suit the envious, feeble-purposed Ferdinand.

CHAPTER III

In the early days of modern spiritualism the sitters expected somewhat strong fare in the matter of spirit phenomena ; and the mediums gave it them in the shape of noisy physical demonstrations and the materialisation of spirit forms. But this side of the business, whilst lucrative, was at times somewhat risky ; and after numerous exposures of the methods by which these physical wonders were worked, and the capture of incautious mediumistic controls masquerading as spirit forms, the mediums deemed it wise to drop a phase of phenomena attended by such obvious risks, and to adopt a phase of the supernatural which eliminated risks of this character and was just as sure a money-getter.

One of the first mediums to be tripped up in London whilst masquerading as a spirit form was an ingenious young lady named Florrie Corner. Her captors were two young friends of mine, undergraduates of Christ Church, Oxford. As the spirit had next to nothing on when she came within the investigators' grasp, the modesty of her youthful captors suffered a rude shock.

Now this medium was a shining light in

spiritualism, and had been endorsed by an eminent scientist, of whose belief in spiritism much is made even to-day.

This scientist evidently found the medium most convincing, and in his writings he went into quite unscientific raptures over a spirit which used to materialise under her control for his scientific undoing. He tells us how this spirit came to him with all the entrancing charms of celestial existence, and he goes on to ask what else could he—or any other mortal under such circumstances—do than take this lovely spirit in his arms ? What indeed ?

But, as I said on the stage of the Savoy, which theatre Sir W. S. Gilbert, Sir Arthur Sullivan, and Mr D'Oyley Carte had placed at my disposal, at the time of the confession of this touching incident, a scientist who indulged in philanderings of this nature—however great the provocation —was much too far gone for proper scientific investigation, and, to my mind, aroused strong doubts as to his strictly scientific impartiality.

For my own part, I have not yet folded a lovely spirit in my arms, and so cannot at first hand say what the sensation is like. But I have at séances seen male sitters embrace feminine visitors from the other world, and, so far as I have been able to judge in the dim light prevailing, the pleasure has been reciprocal. But then in each instance the embracer has been—so at least it was given out—related to the embraced. In the case, however, of the eminent scientist and his winsome spirit no relationship whatever existed. It was just a case of spiritual affinity. If it be possible for such a condition of things to have existence in that other world of the spiritists, this particular " cuddleable " spirit would appear to have been a somewhat forward young thing.

Round about the time my young 'Varsity friends tripped up the winsome spirit " Marie," materialised under the Corner mediumship, I was myself engaged in attending séances where materialisations were a feature.

A very prominent medium for this class of " manifestation " was a German-American named Bastian. I thought the manifestations produced under his mediumship somewhat "thin " ; but in the eyes of the faithful they were considered exceedingly "powerful." The thinness of them I was able to practically demonstrate ; and these are the methods I adopted.

Previous observation had convinced me that if an inquirer ever succeeded in grasping an appearing form there was every possibility of its breaking away during the prevailing excitement, and with the active assistance of the protecting faithful. So, before going to the séance, I took with me a ring syringe filled with liquid cochineal. My idea was to squirt the colouring matter into the face of any form that might appear, at the first favourable opportunity, arguing that a " form " so coloured, should it escape my grasp, would, if a genuine spirit, simply return to its celestial habitation, with, I hoped, as little personal resentment as possible.

But if it were—as I frankly expected it would

be—the medium himself, masquerading as a spirit, then the escape of the form from my grasp would make no difference to the result, as the medium, presumably lying in a " trance condition " behind the thick black curtains, would, on examination, be found to bear traces of the colouring matter on his own face.

It all happened as I anticipated. The form appeared and was duly cochinealed. It escaped, and then followed the examination of the medium, whose face bore distinct traces of the red matter thrown on that of the spirit.

Mr Punch at the time neatly summed up the incident as follows :—

" COTCHING A SPIRIT.

" Bravo, Mr Cumberland !
   Spirits are as slippery as eels to feel,
   So would you cotch a spirit-cochineal ? "

The faithful, reading my account of the affair, published first in the *Daily Chronicle*, and duly condemning my cruelty and irreverence, did not deny the correctness of my claims. " Anyone who knows anything about the subject," they argued, " must know that a form to be materialised has to borrow the materio-spiritual atoms of the medium with which to build up its materialisation, so that any colouring matter thrown on the face of a form would, on that form's dematerialisation, be carried with that dematerialisation back to the body of the medium, from whom the component parts of the materialisation were borrowed."

In just the same way, I suppose, a highly

classical spirit—Dante, to wit—who, on its appearance at an American séance, trod on the business ends of some tin-tacks scattered on the floor of the séance room, carried, on its dematerialisation, the tacks with their excruciating mundane presence back to the feet of the controlling medium, who, under the influence of the pain caused by this dematerialisation process, altogether forgot for the moment that he was manifesting as Dante. His cursing, admittedly excusable under the circumstances, was not, however, in the pure Florentine to be expected, but burst forth in broad and lurid Yankee, which was the medium's own mother tongue.

Mediums, surely, ought to be able to talk the language of the forms they profess to materialise, as well as possess a reasonable degree of artistic accuracy in connection with the outward make-up.

I had begun to look upon Bastian as a back number in the spiritistic world, when news reached me that he was in Vienna, and that the Crown Prince Rudolph, who had heard of my experience with the man, was anxious to know what steps to take to guard against imposture.

My answer was : " Take the necessary precautions to ensure the capture of any spirit form that may appear, and, with the capture of the spirit, you will have the medium."

The outcome was the holding of a séance in the palace of the Archduke Johann (John Orth, of tragic fate), at which the Crown Prince was present. It was so arranged that, when a spook should appear from behind the curtains cloaking the anteroom into which the medium was to retire for the purpose of working up the material- isation, a string should be pulled, fastening the door suddenly behind it with a snap. All the other doors being closed, and the windows fastened, there was no possibility of any appear- ing form escaping, unless it chose to vanish into thin air, in accordance with historic custom. A form did appear ; snap went the spring on the door, and the spirit felt itself trapped. It ran wildly about the room, vainly seeking for some avenue of escape. I am assured that it cut an exceedingly pitiful figure. It goes without say- ing that the spirit was the medium, and, having demonstrated the fraudulent character of the mani- festations, the Imperial captors had to decide what to do with the exposed medium. Eventually it was decided that he should be released, and ejected he was, with his cowering spirit-honours full upon him, with the scantiest ceremony. Bastian wasted no time in leaving Vienna, and a becoming respect for the police authorities caused him to give the Austrian capital a wide berth in future.

So hurried was the hapless medium's departure from the palace that he went in his socks, leaving behind, in the anteroom, the boots he had doffed when coming forth as a noiseless " spook."

These boots, I would add, remained for a long while after at the Hofburg, and when I was there the Crown Prince and Crown Princess begged of me to exercise my powers of thought-reading in the direction of finding the " spirit," and having them returned to him, as the medium, for obvious reasons, was not himself a caller for the lost property.

As the Crown Princess Stephanie added with a smile, " Poor thing, it might get chilblains in this dreadfully cold weather without them ! "

The old Emperor, Francis Joseph, was exceedingly annoyed at the publicity given to the *exposé*. He thought it undignified for a Hapsburg to receive a medium, who certainly was not court-worthy, in order to produce a spirit who might be equally uncourt-worthy, according to strict Austrian court etiquette. It was, I believe, the attitude the independent and impetuous Archduke Johann assumed over the matter that gave rise to the first difference between him and the Emperor. Spiritualists have professed to see in the unknown end of the Archduke and the tragedy of Myerling, with the mystery attached to the death of the Crown Prince, the vengeance of the gods over the outrage offered the manifesting spirit at the archducal palace.

These worthy believers prophesied a sad fate for me too when I exposed the same medium. But, in my case, there was much more to answer for. I did get some tell-tale red marks on my spirit, whereas the Austrian princes simply annexed their ghostly visitor's boots, which had been hurriedly left behind as being of no further use.

Under the blessings or curses of those who have resented my *exposés* I have continued to exist, and long enough, too, to write this book.

. . . .

A cigarette case, lying on my table as I write, recalls an incident of importance connected with the Myerling tragedy. The cigarette case was a present from Baron Nathaniel Rothschild, of Vienna, and was a souvenir of a distinguished artistic gathering I attended in the Austrian capital. At this reception I met for the first time the young Baroness Vetsera, who was to exercise such a fateful influence over the heir to the Austrian throne. She did not make any great impression upon me ; and, to tell the truth, I could not quite understand the Crown Prince's infatuation, which was then in the bud. In appearance she was just an ordinary type of Viennese " flapper," of a somewhat dreamy, romantic temperament. In the experiment I performed with her, she did not indicate any great mental concentration or fixedness of purpose. Indeed, as a " subject," she did not favourably compare with the Crown Princess Stephanie, with whom, at the Hofburg, I had successfully executed some interesting experiments.

The Crown Prince and Crown Princess were never a well-matched pair. They had not two thoughts in common. She, a tall, well-developed blonde, seemed, as she stood by his side, to physically overshadow him. Mentally he was undoubtedly her superior ; but he had not her animal spirits or her latent will power. Whilst mentally lazy, she was active physically. It may have been the contrast in the two women that caused the Crown Prince to lean towards the weaker-willed and more supple Vetsera girl. The attachment awoke fierce resentment on the part of the Crown Princess, who appealed to the Emperor, who, for once in a way, was disposed to side with her.

It was this fierce opposition that brought about the final tragedy. Had it been left to run its course, that course, I am inclined to think, would have been comparatively brief and uneventful. And the truth about that tragedy ? Has the true story ever been told ? Not in print, so far as I have read the various highly imaginative and contradictory reports which have found their way into newspapers and books. All the talk about political plots, of masked plotters, of hired assassins, and the revenge of an outraged wife, are so much rubbish.

The only person who knew the true story first hand and brought it to England and related it to King Edward (then Prince of Wales) was Prince Philip of Coburg. Just before this the same story had reached me from Vienna. It was to the effect that, at this farewell meeting at Myerling, the young baroness had taken poison and the Crown Prince had shot himself.

About the time of Prince Philip's journey of communication Mr Joseph Sebag-Montefiore was giving a house-warming at his newly erected residence near Broadstairs, and, together with Sir Henry Irving and others famous in art, science, and literature, I had the honour of being invited. Sir Henry and I stayed at the Grand Hotel, Broadstairs, as the house itself was full. We had many talks together on that occasion ; and one had reference to the Myerling mystery, around which discussion still raged.

Sir Henry asked me if I, from my somewhat close acquaintance with the principals interested therein, heard the true story of the tragedy. I told him how the story had come to me from Vienna.

" And that is the true one," he said. " I had it yesterday from H.R.H., and he had it from Prince Philip of Coburg, who was present at Myerling."

.   .   .   .   .   .

In Providence, Rhode Island, I once saw a credulous old gentleman present a spirit with a magnificent ring for conveyance to his wife in Spiritland. The next day I saw the medium, who, to my mind at the time, had borne a remarkable likeness to the " form " that had appeared, wearing the same ring on her own hand. I reckoned that it had never left the finger on which the dear old widower had so confidingly placed it the night before.

On another occasion the spirit-wife herself appeared, and sat for a moment upon the mundane knees of the credulous husband. His arms, in the dim light, as in the case of the un-scientific scientist I have mentioned, were soon around her. It may have been all right for the favoured believer, but it was somewhat embar-rassing for the other sitters. Personally, I felt exceedingly uncomfortable, and thought such demonstrations should be reserved for private consumption.

I have no hesitation in saying that materialisations of this character under professional mediumship are rank imposture and form an exceptionally cruel phase of deception. No one knows better than the mediums themselves the full extent of the imposture. Knowing this, they have ever resented the adoption on the part of investigators of precautions which would either lay bare their chicaneries or prohibit the productions altogether.

It surely should be a matter beyond question that if a spirit could effect an appearance on earth, it would appear to those nearest and dearest to it, and not through the agency of a professional or non-professional medium, of whose existence such spirit, whilst previously in earth life, presumably had no knowledge whatever.

With those who claim to have had a first sign direct, and who consult mediums with the object of obtaining further signs and information, it is just a matter of self-deception. The sign-seekers mistake subjective forms for objective. And that is really all there is to it.

Of this psychological phase of spiritism more anon.

Sir Arthur Conan Doyle, who, somehow or other, has managed to get in touch with a feminine spirit, for whose veracity he vouches, claims, on the testimony of this spirit, that the other-worlders have physical feelings and enjoyments, not the least of which, to the female section thereof, is the wearing of clothes.

The information in this direction so far furnished does not go far enough.

For instance, I would like to know if, allowing the existence of physical feelings in celestial form, there is production of population in that other world into which the distinguished novelist has been permitted to obtain so close a glimpse.

I do not ask this idly. From what has been advanced by spiritualistic enthusiasts, one would like to know if the bigamy laws ruling here are run on similar lines in that other world.

In making a point of this, I have in mind the solemn assertion of an ecstatic American believer that not only has his wife returned to him from Spiritland, but that materio-spiritual offspring—on the Gilbertian basis of half a human and half a fairy—have been the outcome of such visits. And there are those in the movement who agree with the possibility of it.

After this the curtain.

CHAPTER IV

PHYSICAL PHENOMENA : TABLE TAPPING, SPIRIT
RAPPING, SLATE WRITING, AND OTHER MORE
OR LESS NOISY FORMS OF "SPIRIT MANI-
FESTATIONS"

MODERN spiritism came in with an atmosphere
that was far more material than spiritual. The
phenomena associated with the earlier séances
were invariably crude, and frequently somewhat
vulgar, in character. Table tipping and rapping
were the most affected forms of communication
between the two worlds.

After sitting under various more or less minor
mediums for manifestations of this character, without receiving one convincing bit of evidence of
the spiritual origin of the manifestations vouchsafed me, I considered myself fortunate in securing
a special sitting with Mrs Fox-Kane, the High
Priestess of the "New Dispensation." The sitting
took place in my apartments at the Everett House,
New York, and people well known in literature,
science, and society were present.

It was the same old thing over again, with the
accepted code of signs and communications, with
its one rap or tip of the table for No ; two raps
or tips for Don't know or Doubtful ; three for

5

Yes or Affirmative ; and five signifying the call for the alphabet, when, from A to Z, questions were put to the dear spirits.

The proceedings at the séance worked out something like this :—

Inquirer : " Dear spirits, are you here ? "

One rap or tip, evidencing the fact that the celestial controls were not there. But how a spirit could signify its absence by a physical indication of its immediate presence has always been beyond me. This form of contradiction is emphasised by the spirit's reply with two tips of the table or two raps in answer to an inquiry as to its presence. Surely the spirit should know whether it was present or not. There ought to be no indefiniteness on this point. And the reader may well comprehend one's disappointment, not unmixed with surprise, when, on asking if a spirit be present, he gets, in spirit language, the information that it doesn't know.

The one person with whom certainty on this point would rest would be the medium ; but with credulous or ingenuous sitters uncertainty is quite a good card to play. It arouses expectancy, and makes room for the more definite indications which may follow.

There is no indefiniteness about the indications when the spirit elects to declare its presence. Then the raps are loud and rapid, unless the spirit be very young or old, when there is less vigour about the demonstration. There is quite an appropriate *piano* touch to the rappings of immature or aged spirits. The mediums insist

upon this distinction, and your true believers
accept it without question.

Now, in the case of the High Priestess of the
New Dispensation, as with the lesser mediumistic
lights whose séances I had attended, no new facts
were brought forward, no proofs of genuine spirit
power were in any way demonstrated.

The tipping of the table was the outcome of
the conscious or unconscious pressure of the hands
placed upon it. It responded to that pressure
and gave the indications which were assumed to
be the outcome of spirit presence or influence.
It was all most material.

And the spirit rapping? The spirits had no
more to do with the sounds produced than had
the man in the moon. They, as some not believing in spirit power would assume, were not
the outcome of mechanical appliances hidden in
the room or manipulated by the medium or a
confederate or secreted on their person. The
rappings, though decidedly non-spiritual, were
directly associated with the medium, and were
of materio-mediumistic as distinct from spirito-
mediumistic origin. Mrs Fox-Kane had certain
physical qualifications which enabled her to produce sounds which were attributed to spirit
power. The dislocation of her fingers, with the
elbow resting on the table or against the wain-
scotting behind acting as a sounding-board, was
one, and the displacement of the *peroneus longus*
muscle of the foot or the ball of the big toe on
the floor under the table was another. I, possessing very similar physical qualifications, have

both in private and in public demonstrated this evidence of " spirit power " in the same manner and under precisely similar conditions to those governing the spirit manifestations of this description as produced through the mediumship of Mrs Fox-Kane and other gifted beings claiming to be endowed with spiritistic powers.

I am fully aware that those who are out for belief alone will not accept this explanation or be convinced by a practical demonstration thereof. But with those who are superior alike to logic and common sense there is no arguing.

These worthy folk will gravely assure you they have heard raps when no medium has been officiating, and the sounds they have thus heard can alone have been the outcome of spirit power or spirit presence.

There is nothing so deceptive as sound ; and the hearing of voices and other sounds, for which a supernatural origin is frequently claimed, is an only too frequent form of hallucination. By a very simple experiment it is quite easy to demonstrate practically the impossibility of anyone, no matter how keen of hearing, locating the exact direction of sound unless the eye is able to see what causes it.   This I have demonstrated the world over, blind people being the only ones who have located the direction with anything approaching accuracy.

With respect to table tipping, one meets people who assert with much positiveness, and occasionally with no little heat, that there has been no pressure on the table on their part, the table in its movements acting through a force quite outside themselves.   So at least, being honest folk, they really think.   But they are self-deceived. The muscular pressure on their part is there, but it is done quite unconsciously.   In such matters the result of unconscious pressure is the same as that of conscious pressure ; but whilst with the former it is easy with those that way inclined to invest the movements with a supernatural origin, the purely mundane character of them is obvious in the case of the latter.

Many years ago an eminent medical friend of mine worked out with me the construction of a simple little machine which duly registered on a tell-tale smoked glass plate every unconscious movement betrayed by anyone who might avow that he had exercised no pressure or given any physical indication when engaged in tests associated with such manifestations as table tipping and turning.   I had a diagram of this machine with explanatory notes printed in the *Pall Mall Gazette*, at which period Mr W. T. Stead, its editor, had not " gone over " to spiritualism. Indeed, Mr Stead, who detested shams and pretences of any kind, was an indignant opponent of the chicaneries and hanky-panky only too frequently associated with spiritistic practices.   He was a man who was for ever trying to get to the bottom of things, and his enthusiasm was liable to get the better of his judgment.

As a psychologist I think I had some interest for him, and he followed my work with close attention and much kindly appreciation.

On one occasion he sought to put my thought-reading experiments to the most exacting tests, and invited to the old *Pall Mall Gazette* offices a number of eminent people, including Sir E. Ray Lankester and Mr Andrew Carnegie, to supervise the experiments. One of the tests was to take a member of the audience and find something thought of that was quite away from the building. Mr Grant Allen, the novelist, was the subject for the experiment, and, blindfolded, I led him from the room out into the street through a wondering crowd of mixed humanity. We paused at a house. A loud knock brought a woman to the door. On opening it, and seeing a blindfolded man grasping another man by the wrist attended by a small nondescript following of men, women, and children, she apparently wondered what was up, and muttered something about fetching a policeman. But someone assured her it was all right, and we entered the passage, and I took my " subject " upstairs, and, in a box in a room there, I found the object thought of. It turned out to be the well-preserved piece of workhouse bread the late Mr Greenwood had received when filling the rôle of the " Amateur Casual." I took the trophy back to the *Gazette* office, and no one was more warm in his appreciation of the success of the experiment than Mr Stead.

The next morning, as I was sauntering by Charing Cross, a street arab looked at me with evident admiration.

" See that bloke ? " said he to a small urchin by his side.

" Yus."

" Know 'im ? "

" Naw."

" Well, that's the cove as broke inter that 'ouse over there and pinched a bit o' all right as 'ad bin planted there."

" Did 'e, now !—an' what did 'e get ? "

" Nothin', yer silly. It was all play-actin'."

This story highly amused Stead, who used to say that had I lived in the times of the Inquisition I would for a certainty have ended my days at the stake, and that I was lucky to have been born in an age when Science understood and endorsed what was so perfectly natural, but which an ignorant past would at once have classed as black magic.

And this liberal-minded, highly intelligent man went over to modern spiritism, with its incentives to self-deception and possibilities of false sensorial impressions ! The pity of it !

With this temporary diversion I return to the subject of physical phenomena.

I have frequently been assured by those who, whilst their judgment might be open to question, were by nature veracious, that they had seen a table indulge in movements when not in contact with the human form, such movements being the outcome of its own strange volition or the result of spirit influence. The late King Edward used to tell a highly-amusing story respecting the fantastic movements of a table while under so-called spirit influence. The telling of it, in cold print, would spoil it.

Tables have ever declined to manifest in this mysterious manner in my presence alone or when those who claim to have been previously favoured in this direction were present. This I have always thought to be somewhat uppish on the part of the tables themselves, or distinctly unkind of the spirits who were assumed to influence them. There has, therefore, been nothing left me, in the absence of the direct proof required of its actual occurrence, but to raise my eyebrows wonderingly at the extent of some sign-seekers' imagination. True, I have seen a table glide across a room, seemingly without human contact. It at first puzzled me, as the agency responsible for the movement, although surely not spiritual, was certainly not visible. The table, I noted, went only one way—in the direction of the medium. That was accounted for by the fact that the medium was the only one in the room who controlled the spirit influence, and to her the table, feeling the influence, obviously would move.

I agreed that the medium was the attraction. Indeed she was, but not in the way the believers figured.

The table came to her because she was connected with it by a piece of invisible Chinese silk thread. At each end of the thread was a bent pin. One pin was attached to her shoe, and the other was fixed to the table when she passed her hands over it invoking the influence of the dear spirits. When she sat down and, covered by her skirts, manipulated the thread, the spirits worked and the table moved on its castors.

A castorless table would have done a wobble, but the spiritual glide would have been off.

This was bold, bad conjuring; and, as far as possible, the most conscienceless professional medium avoids mere vulgar sleight-of-hand aids in working his phenomena, with the consequent risk of being tripped up. But to move tables without contact a little conjuring has to be brought in.

Knowing, as they do to the full, that no reliance whatever can be placed upon spirit assistance in the matter of the production of physical phenomena, the professional medium has to rely solely upon his own ingenuity and adroitness. That is why the manifestations are of such an earthly character. Being, as they are, the outcome of human conception and manipulations, they could not well be otherwise.

If even the most credulous of sign-seekers had for a single moment given this aspect of the phenomena which have been provided for their delectation, they, I think, could not but arrive at the one conclusion, that spirits should be better employed in that other world of theirs than in visiting this in order to demonstrate their spiritual existence by methods which would be more appropriate to a booth in a country fair.

These professional mediums have produced phenomena according to their lights, making as much as possible out of their dupes in the process. It, therefore, would be unfair to blame the spirits for the vulgarity and sheer banality of the manifestations provided at so many séances, with which "manifestations" they, as a matter of fact, have neither connection nor knowledge.

Oh, those vulgarities, those banalities, how they have wearied me, angered me, and disgusted me!

There was at one time a prominent medium who held forth in the Bloomsbury district. He specialised in dark séances ; and the chief " spirit guide," who manipulated under his control, was one John King. In earth-life John King, according to his own story, had followed the calling of a buccaneer, and though since his transformation to Spiritland he had become refined, he still retained a good deal of that roughness of voice and manner which one would be disposed to associate with his earthly existence. It is not impossible that he may have been the ancestor of a piratical U-boat commander. He, so far as I am aware, never indulged in "full form" materialisations at these séances, contenting himself with a mere profile visitation on such occasions as this limited aspect of materialisation was considered safe. A " spirit photo " of him full face showed him to be of swarthy complexion, with a full black beard, and a sort of white turban headgear. But a sight of even this abbreviated portion of his engaging spiritual personality was denied me at every séance I attended, although on more than one occasion there were those present who vowed they could see him, a phosphorescent glow in the darkness, as well as feel his strong spiritual presence. But on several occasions he signified his presence by speaking through a paper tube, placed upon the table by the medium for the purpose, in a singularly husky and surly voice.

The first time he "manifested" in this way I was told in a whisper by a lady sitting next me that the spirit of John King was present.

"Are you John King?" I asked with becoming solemnity.

"I are," replied the spirit. In questioning this form of reply one must take into consideration that on earth John King's education had been neglected, and that he had not at that period apparently gone through that phase of spiritual progress—which I assume is educational as well as physical—spoken of with such certainty by your true believer.

A distinguished scientist who had accompanied me to the séance was highly tickled at the spirit's lapse in grammar, and his laugh, in its heartiness, was, I must admit, singularly inappropriate for a dark séance devoted to obtaining manifestations from the other world. Before the sitters had recovered from the shock caused by his hearty laugh my friend broke in with, "John King? No, my dear spirit, you are not John King; you surely are *Jo* King."

Needless to say, this disturbed the harmony of the séance to the extent of bringing it to an abrupt termination. We were told by the medium in solemn, injured tones there would be no more manifestations that night. The spirits, it appears, resent anything approaching levity, although "John King" on more than one occasion banged sitters on the heads with the stiff paper tubes, through which he was allowed to speak, after the manner of a hardened knockabout.

At these sittings there was always music on tap, produced through the instrumentality of a large-sized musical box, which the manifesting spirits wound up—*in the dark*. This musical box was carried round the room by, it was alleged, " spirit power." One could hear it bumping against the ceiling or knocking against the walls and door in its passage round the room. I was much concerned as to the fate of the sitters should the heavy box slip from the hands of the officiating spook and drop in the darkness in their midst. In such case it was a moral certainty that the " evil spirits," who creep into these circles when an investigator, as distinct from a believer, is present, would have taken note of my own position in the circle. It was therefore some relief to my conjectural apprehensions when the floating musical box was carried out of the room by the officiating spirit. One could hear the music it provided growing more and more muffled, until in its faintness it seemed to be outside the room altogether. Then the box would return to the séance room by degrees in the same muffled-up way, and finally, with a loud bump, would be re-deposited on the table from whence it, in the first instance, had been removed by the spirit power prevailing at the sitting.

Then the lights went up, and one was at liberty to gaze at will upon the box, which in spirit hands had, in its aerial flight, so gravely affected the safety of the sitters.

In these days of air raids, when one sits in a darkened room wondering if the murderous enemy airman will drop a bomb upon us, one's thoughts go back to that dark séance, with the musical box bomb poised above one's head ; and as one to-day eagerly awaits the " All clear " bugle, so in those past days did I with not unnatural eagerness welcome the word " *Lights !* " and the letting in of light upon our darkness.

It goes without saying that neither John King nor any other visitor from the Beyond wound up the musical box or carried it in its bumping career around the room.   It was all due to purely human agency—that of the medium.   He wound up the box at the start, lifted it up and whirled it around to represent its movements by spirit force.   In the darkness one could not see what was being done ; one could only hear and make the best calculations under the circumstances as to the direction of the sound.

The medium was a cadaverous, dour-looking person, but he had a big hand and a strong wrist.   This was in his favour when it came to lifting and making movements with a heavy weight, such as was that particular musical box.

When the box was supposed to be carried out of the room by the spirit the medium commenced sitting upon it ; and when its muffled, far-off sounds indicated that it had left the room, *the medium was sitting full upon it.*   Anyone with a musical box can reproduce this phenomenon under precisely similar conditions to those laid down by the medium and accepted by the believers as guaranteeing the existence of spirit control.

After several sittings, during which I discovered how the medium freed his hands from those who were confident they were in close physical contact with him the whole time, in order to manipulate the musical box, I determined to so arrange matters that the proof of the power winding up the box and what followed would be placed beyond question. So, after the turning out of the lights on the sitters clasping hands round the table on which had been placed the box preparatory to the commencement of the manifestations, I, in the darkness, smeared some lamp-black on the handle of the box. It was wound up, and the customary meanderings around the room followed. Seldom before had I followed a spirit manifestation with such interest. How I longed for the word " Lights ! " in order to see the outcome of my plan ! How I trembled at the thought of the spirit making a discovery of the little trap I had set, and by way of recognition of my zeal dropping the heavy box on my head ! At last there was light on our darkness, and upon the medium's right hand, which was lamp-blacked to an extent that would carry conviction to the blindest as to whose agency the winding up of the box was due. But that was not all. The surface of the box itself was smeared through contact with the black greasy hand, and some of the stuff was on the seat of the medium's trousers, where he had sat upon the instrument during its disappearance from the room under spirit control.

Were the believers convinced by this un-answerable *exposé*? Not a bit of it. An evil spirit had crept into the circle and had sought to injure the poor medium—a good old con-vincing tag to trot out is the "evil spirit" theory. As for myself, boiling in oil would be a minor form of punishment according to my deserts. I was lucky enough to leave that séance in safety.

But investigating the occult I have found at times somewhat hazardous, and more than once my life itself has been in danger.

At Boston, in America, a leading light of the spiritistic cause, one Dr Bliss, drew a gun on me for interfering with the smooth working of one of the most fraudulent séances I have ever attended. In the course of a violent struggle one of my assailants had his skull cracked and I got a dislocated ankle. For some time I lay in bed under very kindly medical supervision with the dislocated ankle reposing in a pillow cradle, during which period the medium and his associates bombarded me with notes written in red ink, in which the early close of my earthly career was predicted. The final note contained the rough drawing of a coffin—studded with red nails, by the by—with the explanation that this was the sort of box in which alone I should leave my hotel. The police were called in, and during my public representations at the Tremont Temple which followed, I, in a way, was under police pro-tection. In this country such a man as Dr Bliss would have been promptly arrested for threatening to murder ; but in the States, being a Britisher, I was in the eyes of the law an alien, and, being an alien, I was required to find very substantial bond in connection with a prosecution of this character. How the " dear spirits " must have rejoiced at the dilemma in which I found myself ! They were free to carry on their highly profitable little hanky-pankyisms without interference from me, lying *hors de combat* at the hotel ; and the law, as I was due to appear in Canada and so could not furnish the bond required, was unable to help me.

But to even the hopelessly sinful, such as myself, there comes earthly satisfaction at times. It came eventually in the arrest of the bellicose Bliss. My *exposé* of his fraudulent practices as a medium had drawn the attention of the police to him, and investigations which followed disclosed that his séance room was a den of iniquity. It had been the road to ruin of many a young and innocent schoolgirl. For his offences against society Bliss received a sentence of ten years. I don't know if the spirits he controlled whilst at liberty to extract money out of dupes and lead youth to its moral undoing gave him a helping hand whilst in prison. By this time he is doubtless himself a spirit ; and, as Sir Arthur Conan Doyle lays it down that evil humans, when they are transferred to Spiritland, take with them all their evil characteristics, it would be rough on any self-respecting spirit to have to associate for even the briefest transitory period with the spiritual part of so evil a character as Bliss.

Slate writing, like rope tying and cabinet manifestations, has gone out of fashion in the spiritistic world.

The exposure of the notorious Dr Slade by Sir E. Ray Lankester and Sir Horatio Donkin killed the former phase of spirit phenomena in this country, and Sir Henry Irving and Mr John L. Toole's *exposé* of the tricks of the Davenport Brothers destroyed any lingering belief in the genuineness of this class of physical manifestation.

The last time I met Dr Slade was in a small town in Ontario, where he had been exposed by an intelligent young Canadian journalist.

Slade worked the slate-writing oracle by changing the slates. It is generally performed on a basis of legerdemain. He knew well the art of distracting attention whilst arranging the changes, and he could simulate the scratching, supposed to be the work of the pencil point guided by spirit power, between the locked slates, to perfection. He was a clever artist, and in these days, when spirit messages are so much in favour among the sign-seekers, would have so arranged his tactics to meet the new conditions as to have taken in those sign-endorsing folk, whose policy seems to be to accept without proof anything that comes along as an instance of spirit existence.

Whilst modern spiritualism, as we know it, came in with the two Fox girls, the mediums who followed drew upon the Red Indians for their inspiration in the production of the more rough-and-tumble physical phenomena.

The medicine men of the various tribes out

6

West were adepts at the game long before the centres of art and culture were asked to witness demonstrations of spirit power.

In order to impress the tribe in accordance with its mystic leanings the medicine men elected to be bound by the strong men of the tribe in such a fashion that no known earthly method could release them. When the officiating medicine men had succeeded in releasing themselves, they demonstrated the fact by noisy illustrations inside the *tepee* in which they were bound. Instruments were blown and objects thrown through openings in the tent. This the onlookers accepted as evidence of magic.

I have, whilst out West, seen demonstrations of this character, and I thought it very good " magic." Indeed, as a magic show it surpassed the very best illustrations of so-called spirit power displayed through the mediumship of the most gifted being claiming association with the other world. And the test conditions prevailing at the séances on the prairie were certainly more stringent than those appertaining to an avowed spiritistic sitting.

As will be seen, the *tepee* of the Red Indian became the cabinet of the spirit medium, with kindred manifestations for the bewilderment of the onlookers. But no medium ever admitted that he had borrowed his tricks from the Red Man ; and it will, I fancy, be somewhat painful to the out-and-out believers in modern spiritualism that manifestations which so convincingly reflect evidence of spirit existence in that other world of theirs had their origin on *terra firma*, with pagan Redskins as the exponents thereof.

The spirit mediums of the West, in the matter of mysticism, have much to learn from the East. There is a wide difference between the supernaturalism of the West and the occultism of the East, and in character and pretence they have no place in that other world of spiritualistic imagination.

On another occasion I may deal expressly with the occultism of the East, which I have somewhat closely investigated.

CHAPTER V

THE CLAIMS AND CHICANERIES OF CLAIRVOYANCE

CLAIRVOYANCE has ever formed an important branch of occultism, and to-day, in connection with so-called " spirit " manifestations, is quite a leading feature.

I have had an exceedingly wide experience of the gifted beings—of both sexes—claiming clairvoyant powers ; and here, too, I must say I have not been fortunate enough to witness any one illustration that was not explicable on a basis widely removed from supernatural agencies.

Some of the features demonstrated for my delectation have been rank imposture, whilst others had their origin and their finish in mere conjecture.

In the early days of the spiritistic movement the " clairvoyant reading " of names and messages written on slips of paper folded up into squares or placed in closed-up envelopes was a common item at séances, and mediums on the make still practise this form of chicanery.

It was an effective feature when skilfully performed ; but as it was the outcome of un-diluted trickery, the mediums ran the risk of being bowled over whilst ringing the changes of the slips, on which the names of the " departed " had been written by the inquirer.   It was not long before I discovered the *modus operandi* of this form of " clairvoyant power," and I was able to duplicate the feats by the same means and under the same conditions as those under which they were produced as genuine instances of supernaturalism.   This was one of the many duplications of spirit manifestations I satisfactorily demonstrated with the eminent scientists and others referred to in my opening chapter, and which I have demonstrated in public before very large audiences in various parts of the world.   Whilst a commonsense public has seen in this illustration an unanswerable *exposé* of supernatural pretensions, there have not been lacking out-and-out believers in spiritism who have claimed for me a gift like that of the mediums whom I sought to overthrow, and that I preferred my way of demonstrating because it had the advantage of being more popular.   Others of the cult, whilst admitting my possession of the mediumistic or clairvoyant gift, explained my own ignorance of its possession to my gross materialism and wilful perversity.

But to be both grossly materialistic and wilfully perverse appears to me to have distinct moral advantages over fraudulent pretences, no matter by whom practised or by whom believed in.

At times I had not a little fun at these séances ; for, when one is convinced that the whole thing is mere hanky-panky, it is surely permissible to give the more humorous side of things a show, it being for the spiritual influences controlling the sittings to separate the wheat from the chaff as might be considered best. So, when I was asked to write the names of departed spirit friends with whom I would like to be placed in communication, I was, at times, moved to write those indicating certain Scotch and Irish spirits with whom I had been out of touch for many years. In that sense they were among the departed.

On touching with the end of her pencil the pellet containing, for instance, the name of Johnny Walker, the medium would ask, "Dear spirit, are you here?" And if the one rap reply came, signifying "No," it obviously brought disappointment; with the two raps—"Don't know"—would arise a desire for greater certainty on the spirit's part; whilst with a three rap—"Yes"—rejoinder one's thoughts would run in the direction of the immediate materialisation of a tumbler and siphon.

In connection with my inquiries as to my Scotch and Irish spirit friends, in not one instance did a medium ever succeed in accurately describing the age or particulars of the spirit evoked, although he or she, by the process I have named, had managed to get at the name I had written down.

Poor Johnny Walker! how sadly he has been caricatured in the descriptions furnished by the mediumistic clairvoyantes, who have pretended to get in touch with a spirit of that name, and who, with all their clear far-seeingness, were unable to give the faintest likeness of the engaging personality of one whose pictorial presentment would be so familiar to even the most short-sighted amongst dwellers on this mundane sphere. But in justice to these mediums it should be said that they doubtless did not recognise in the name I had written the much-advertised " Spirit of the Future " !

From experience, I should say that spirit controls have little sense of humour ; or, as I am decidedly of opinion that the real spirit world has no part in the hanky-pankyism prevailing at professional séances, and as everything that occurs thereat is due beyond question to human agency and human ingenuity, it is presiding mediums themselves who are lacking in the saving sense.

Whilst now and again a medium in the manipulation of the papers upon which the names of the departed are written may display an originality that causes a momentary perplexity, the basis of manipulation, as a general thing, is applicable to all séances adopting this form of mystification.

. . . .

But on one occasion, in New York, I came across a medium who adopted entirely new methods, and who for a time puzzled me exceedingly.

His success as a spirit-clairvoyant had caused quite a sensation in the Empire City of the States, and sceptics looked to me for an explanation of the seemingly inexplicable phenomena,

To a séance held under his auspices I took with me two hard-headed investigators of a great daily newspaper. They came to scoff, and remained to pray. For the medium succeeded in every instance with all three of us. In the tests with him the little slips of paper upon which the names were written were not merely folded up in four, and so readily available for mediumistic substitution, but were rolled up by the writer himself firmly into pellets. It was permissible, moreover, to write the names of the living as well as the dead upon the slips ; and when the pellets were mixed together in a little heap by the writer himself, it, to the ordinary observer, seemed impossible to say with any certainty which was which, let alone read the names therein contained. Yet the medium picked out the living from the dead and read their contents with accuracy, though at times somewhat hesitatingly.

My companions were impressed, and I was greatly puzzled. The old solution did not apply to this new form of clairvoyant reading. It was not, I felt assured, the outcome of some real clairvoyant gift. There was abnormal ingenuity, well-conceived hidden trickery somewhere ;— but where ?

The newspaper men went to their office to detail the events and write up the mystic. I returned to my hotel to think deeply all night over the matter and to find a solution. But no satisfactory solution presented itself. The fact that we were asked to put a + against the names of the departed as distinct from the names of the living seemed to me to provide a form of help to the medium, but the point did not go very far in the way of solution.

The next day we all three, as arranged, attended a further demonstration of clairvoyant power. The medium's manner on receiving me, whilst the reverse of hostile, had a pitying sarcasm about it that was not exactly agreeable ; and then, the attitude of my journalistic companions was anything but consoling. They had seen the things the medium had done, and had expressed their views according to how the feats performed had impressed them. As I had not been able to straightway furnish a material explanation of how they were actually performed, they were disposed to back the clairvoyant and look upon me as a solver of mysteries of this character on mundane lines as a failure.

The clairvoyant chuckled inwardly at the impression he saw he had made upon these investigators, and his attitude towards me became increasingly patronising. He suggested I should write down some more names, and, at the same time, take every precaution against his overlooking what I was writing.

The clairvoyant, by the by, had the most remarkable eyes I had ever seen in a human face. They were exceptionally large, and projected somewhat. There was a seemingly luminous touch to them, which suggested mesmeric influence as well as abnormal powers of observation. To make the tests more convincing, he suggested that the names should be written on slips of paper on a table in an anteroom at the end of the séance room in which we were standing.

My companions went there separately and did the writing, and then returned with slips of paper rolled already into pellets, and placed them, one by one, on the table in the séance room. There was no chance of the clairvoyant overlooking the writers, as I stood by his side the whole time the writing was done, and I had dismissed from my calculations any possibility of confederacy, reflection, or the use of tracing paper, associated with some séances of my experience. Yet the medium, by merely touching the pellet with the point of a pencil correctly described its contents. He was, it was true, not so quick as when the names had been written in his presence, and in two instances I noticed that the name was wrongly indicated, although the name itself was there, but on a pellet other than the one at first indicated. He got it all right in the end; but your true clairvoyant ought not in such matters to have two shots at a target. Either he knows what a folded-up piece of paper really contains, or he doesn't. It is not enough, to convey absolute conviction as to clairvoyant powers, to say what a man has written, but it is for him to clairvoyantly reveal with absolute correctness the actual contents of each pellet he sets himself out to decipher through his assumed clairvoyant gifts.

This little blunder caused me to seriously reflect. I saw in it the first stage in a solution of the phenomenon, indicating, as it did, a lapse of observation somewhere.

My time came to write names at that table in the other room. I wrote one and folded the slip of paper into a pellet and set it aside, and then another. When it came to writing down a third there flashed across my mind the remembrance of a thought-reading experiment I had successfully performed with a subject who had thought of a word in Hebrew. The word was Moses ; and so I would give the name of the ancient Lawgiver, as I had done in my own experiment, in Hebrew characters.

With my task finished I returned to the outer room, and laid on the table the pellets in the sequence in which they had been completed.

The clairvoyant read out the first without any hesitancy, and then the second, but when he came to the remaining pellet he paused. "This," he went on, "is the name of one who has long since passed away. He is a very powerful spirit." His voice struck an almost reverential note, and his Hebraic countenance took on a look of additional enthusiasm. "The name you have written is Moses. Is that right ? "

" Quite right," I replied, picking up the pellet.

" And now are you convinced ? " asked the medium as we were leaving.

" I think," I replied, " you have the most remarkable powers of observation and the gift of a trained adjustive memory beyond anything I have ever witnessed."

As I said this he gave me a deep, inquiring look as if searching to find how far I had fathomed his clairvoyant methods.

But I said no more, and passed out with our fellow-inquirers.

"Well," asked one of them, "are you any nearer the solution than before, or have you decided to give him best?"

"Yes, I think I've got the hang of it at last."

"How do you make it?"

"Well, that man has no more real clairvoyant powers than you or I. He has wonderful eye-sight and a most retentive memory. He worked the oracle by *watching the movement of the top of the pencil* with which the names were written. This must have entailed a constant and lengthy practice."

"But how about picking out the names from the pile correctly?"

"You will remember you placed them one by one first in the order they were written. He would remember more or less the position of each; when he didn't, he stumbled."

"But that Moses touch was, I should have thought, a poser. You've got the pellet with you, haven't you? I would like to reproduce it in my account."

I handed him the pellet, which I still retained between my thumb and finger. He opened it.

"Why," he said with marked surprise, "there is nothing written on this slip. It's a blank."

"Exactly," I replied, taking from my pocket the slip on which I had written the word Moses. I explained how, after writing the name, I had substituted the blank pellet for the one I had transferred to my pocket, being convinced that the medium would have observed by his system of observation what I had written, although the writing, being in Hebrew, would be from right to left, and not, as with the other two written in Latin characters, from left to right, and that he would assume the Moses pellet would be included in the three placed by me on the table. Had he been a genuine clairvoyant he would have seen that the pseudo-Moses pellet was a " dud," and so have declared it ; but he was going on astute observation and on memory, and not upon clairvoyance. Neither observation nor memory failed him, but his boasted clairvoyant powers had apparently taken a holiday for the moment.

  .   .   .   .   .

I never saw this clairvoyant medium again, but the experience I had gained with him enabled me to guard against the application of similar gifts exercised by any other member of the mystic fraternity.

Some mystic seers, it should be added, did not claim mediumistic powers together with their clairvoyant gifts, and did not profess to be in that direct touch with Spiritland so boldly asserted by the whole-hoggers of the mediumistic craft. It was enough for them to pose as something mystic, something out of the common, in order to impress the credulous and make money at the same time. They were not so dangerous to the community as the spirit mediums trading upon the sorrows and longings of the bereaved. But whilst, as a rule, they did not do any particular harm, they, it must be confessed, did precious little good. No clairvoyant, within my personal knowledge, has ever told us anything with respect to the unknown that was of any material advantage. Were the gift of clairvoyance real, it, in the possession of an honest, worthy practitioner, might be productive of no little good, telling us something that we might really want to know, and warning us against unseen dangers and disasters untraceable by generally accepted means. But the seers claiming the gift altogether fail us in directions where it might be really usefully employed.

But then the clairvoyant gift, as claimed by some demonstrators and accepted as such by the illogical and impressionable, has no actual existence. Miracles cannot be accomplished in the absence of that force which alone permits of the accomplishment of the miraculous.

It must be admitted that the belief in clairvoyance in some form or other is far more general than a belief in spirit manifestations ; for whereas the former rests the more firmly upon the individual belief that he or she is more gifted than the ordinary, and that things do happen for which no satisfactory explanation outside of the possession of such a gift is apparently forthcoming, outward and visible signs of the latter's existence are apt to be demanded before belief and acceptance can be secured.

The medium of to-day, knowing the risks of exposure attending the production of material manifestations in proof of spirit existence, gives that phase of spirit power a well-earned rest ; and, knowing well his market, adopts the safer plan of spirits—clairvoyant revelations, which, whilst almost as convincing to the expectant sign-seeker, are infinitely safer in that form of presentation.

No risks are entailed in the ecstatic attitudes struck by the medium when contact with that " other world " is being established, or in the volume of wordy piffle giving a description of the life Beyond with the establishment of that contact, beyond the obvious suspicion uppermost in the minds of anyone not obsessed by expectancy and belief that the medium is likely to be more loquacious than veracious, and that he or she is under the suspicion of, as it were, " talking through his hat."

For this line of business female mediums are more effective than male. By nature they are better actors for this particular rôle ; and where closer logical sequence and less irrational meanderings might well be demanded of a male seer, such points would not be the subject of a similar demand in the case of a gifted female. Just as with the medium it is the female element as devotees who count, so in the séance room it is the female control who scores. Whilst we boggle over Woman's Rights in this world, woman's infinite superiority in that other world would appear to be an accepted fact ever since modern spiritualism and all that went with it came in.

Needless to say, the finest and " most convincing " results to-day obtained in connection with other-world communications come through female mediums, possessing, as claimed, clairvoyante as well as mediumistic gifts.

Through such a medium Sir Arthur Conan Doyle has obtained information anent the doings of a highly veracious spirit named Dorothy Postlethwaite. This young lady, being of a highly modest disposition, wears clothes, as do apparently the spirits in the circle in which she mixes. But whether she affects pre-war attire, or that with its high-heeled boots, transparent stockings, and superabundance of furs and jewellery which mark these days of extravagance in feminine adornment, is not stated. This is an omission to be regretted. And whilst Dorothy, or the medium through whom she manifested, was about it, she might have told us how, for instance, Mother Eve was herself attired. It, I think, would have been more satisfactory to have been told that, on translation to the celestial sphere, the feminine mind discarded such mundane weaknesses as dress and fashions.

Another medium with a rich Ouidaesque imagination has, through the agency of that gifted writer Mr Max Pemberton, told us of the spirit of a young officer, killed on the field of battle, who is having no end of a good time in that other world of the controlling medium's imagination. He, we are told, bathes in scented water in an alabaster bath, roves through groves of spreading trees, reclines on a luxurious sofa, or takes his ease in a most comfortable arm-chair. Ouida in her most flamboyant fancy never drew a picture of one of her young heroes' earthly enjoyments that could equal those enjoyed by Mr Max Pemberton's spirit creation. Frankly, I would like to know more about the doings of this spirit. One has been favoured with just enough to whet one's appetite for further adventures and revelations. They smoke, too, in Spiritland—brands not stated, however. Considering the shortage of tobacco in this world, it, verily, is enough to make the inveterate smoker's mouth water to be told there is an abundance of the weed that soothes in that other world, with, apparently, no vexatious Tobacco Control regulations to run one's spiritual head against.

These "seeing mediums" are truly wonderful beings, and it is indeed a thousand pities that one cannot see with their eyes the wonders of the other world which they assert are made so visible to them. The next best thing, according to how you view it, is, I suppose, to accept without question all they tell us as being made so clear to them. But the best plan of all, from the sheer rational, common-sense standpoint, is to decline to believe that this alleged insight into these other-world happenings has any real existence. View the utterings as mere verbal vapourings based upon a highly imaginative and none too scrupulous temperament. In not one instance does the "seeing medium" produce a single scrap of convincing evidence of the existence of the occurrences so glibly depicted.

Professional mediums wilfully deceive without stint for appropriate monetary considerations, wilful deception being a leading item of their

7

stock-in-trade.　Non-professional mediums are out for *kudos*.　They, in the main, must know that they themselves do not possess the powers they are credited with possessing ; but without the assumption of such powers they would be just ordinary folk, and, when a spiritualistic wave is on, to be considered merely ordinary is being out of it.　To the mystically inclined, with the powers of self-deception and the ability to impress others abnormally developed, such a position would be altogether unthinkable.

Whilst the evidence of spirit communications through professional mediumship may well be looked upon as tainted, that arrived at through non-professional mediumship, if less open to question on commercial grounds, to speak quite frankly, is none the more reliable.　For such mediums furnish no proof whatever of their being in possession of powers denied the rest of humanity.　In the absence of the proof of the possession of such powers, what reliance can be placed upon the communications they allege are made through this non-existent mediumship ?

All in all, it simply amounts to this : the majority of " spirit " communications from the other world come through human agency, and, beyond the bare assertion of humans, carry with them no direct evidence of spiritual origin.　No wonder the communications bear traces of the human touch, both in construction and expression.

So much for mediums who rope in the spirits in association with their alleged gifts of clairvoyance.

But a note or two with respect to those who pose as clairvoyants pure and simple, without tacking on spiritistic pretensions.

Some operate as crystal-gazers, some as palmists; and there are others who discard crystals and cards and other fortune-telling adjuncts, and go in for reading the past, present, and future through sheer inspiration.

I have met many who have deceived themselves in assuming a belief that they possessed gifts beyond their fellows, and others who have claimed to have obtained results by means which they themselves knew quite well were the outcome of trickery.

.　　　.　　　.　　　.　　　.

There was once a youth up North who had gained considerable local reputation as a clairvoyant, and I was asked to investigate his claims and furnish an explanation of what—outside of clairvoyance—was said to be altogether inexplicable. Dick, the "Pitboy Clairvoyant," I found to be a very ordinary youth, with about as much clairvoyant power as might reasonably be expected to be contained in the interior anatomy of a Dutch oyster. He was stated to be clairvoyant through his eyebrows, and, in blindfolding him, care had to be taken that his sight-seeing eyebrows were left uncovered. Of course those eyebrows had nothing whatever to do with depicting objects placed over them whilst the blindfolded seer was evoking his clairvoyant powers.

He had funny, cunning little eyes, which, for the purpose of the test, he had the useful knack

of turning upwards and so seeing over the rim
of the blindfold, and thus getting at what was
placed above. Great practice had enabled him
to work the oracle with ease and effect. Whilst
leaving the eyebrows free to work out their clairvoyant mission, my plan was to so obscure the
eyes that the upward movement would be of no
avail. A little wadding in each eye-cup, covered
by a penny, with the bandage over all to keep
the covering in place, completely disposed of the
clairvoyant gift.

What the eyebrows described with accuracy
before the eyes were so covered, they quite failed
to get even the faintest inkling of when my
system of blindfolding was adopted. There was
a good deal of guesswork on the part of the clairvoyant under these conditions, but he was unable
to tumble on to anything approaching a correctness of description any better than the most ordinary individual similarly blindfolded.

The failure of Dick to work the oracle under
proper test conditions promptly disposed of his
claims as a clairvoyant ; and the hard-headed, if
somewhat tender-hearted, Northumbrians resented
the way in which they had been tricked. It will,
I fancy, be some time before Northumbrian miners
in the locality which knew and still remembers
its Pitboy Dick will be subscribing for garlands
with which to deck the brows of local claimants
to supernatural powers.

.   .   .   .   .

I was once asked to visit Cornwall to see quite
a heaven-sent young seeress, who had succeeded

in convincing her unsuspecting father, amongst others, of her possession of extraordinary clairvoyant gifts. Poor father ! I don't think I have ever seen anything quite so cunning in a claimant to occult powers as was personified in this very youthful clairvoyante.

She had all the outward airs of refreshing innocence and truth. It, at first sight, would have seemed a crime to have suspected such a person for a single moment. And yet no one practising the art of occult deception was more deserving of suspicion or required more careful watching. She made every possible, and in certain instances quite extraordinary, use of those simple, truth-speaking eyes of hers in arriving at her clairvoyant conclusions. But when I adopted the sight-obscuring methods, as employed in the case of Dick the Pitboy, nothing but failure was encountered.

She was a very petulant young lady, and her attitude towards me at the employment of these little commonplace methods, in order to set aside the use of gifts other than strictly clairvoyant, was somewhat vixenish. Dear, simple, innocent-looking young thing, this new attitude, however natural, did not become her.

When her father was out of the room, and she felt it better to drop the air of injured innocence, she frankly confided to me that she knew as well as I did she did not possess clairvoyant powers, but that it was so nice to be thought gifted in this way. One then was no longer ordinary ; and to be merely ordinary in life was being really nothing.   Some girls were considered out-of-the-way on account of their proficiency in music, art, or literature—all of them merely normal qualifications.   But clairvoyance was outside of the normal; and, by associating herself with it, she possessed a local interest beyond the common.   Her vanity, evidently, was not a little flattered at the local successes she had achieved.

And her father honestly believed in her gifts, and through him chiefly that belief had obtained credence in the locality in which they resided.

In answer to my query why his gifted daughter had not exercised her art in the direction of giving valuable information in connection with certain mining enterprises with which he was associated : "This is just what she has done," replied this trusting Cousin Jack.   " I had been searching for a missing lode below the third level without success, when she clairvoyantly located it."

And that wholly unsuspecting mine manager would rather believe in the impossible through his daughter—who in this direction at least was unworthy of a moment's credence—than that his own knowledge of mining plus persistent exploration had resulted in the ultimate location of the missing lode !

.   .   .   .   .

By far the cleverest palm-reading clairvoyant of the professional kind I met in the course of my investigations into professional clairvoyance was the original Cheiro, who had attractive chambers in Bond Street.   His lowest fee was one guinea, and I believe he frequently received much larger sums from those with curiosity to satisfy and cash to part with.

Cheiro was a man of the world, and of a really engaging personality. Young girls found him "quite nice," and more elderly dames "most fascinating." He certainly had great success with the fair sex, and the fascination he undoubtedly exercised over them went a long way towards building up the success he achieved in Society. But whilst women formed the majority of his best-paying and most enthusiastic clients, he succeeded in impressing quite a number of well-known and hard-headed public men. The bulky visitors' book, containing the impressions of people of note who had received guidance or uncanny readings at his hands, was quite an interesting volume. I studied it with much attention, and, finally, after his reading of me, wrote therein my impressions of his mystic art. With me he dealt chiefly with the Future—a fairly safe form of prophecy. But this Future, as I pointed out in my letter of impressions, was on the lap of the gods, unreadable by any human being. As a matter of fact, his prophecies with respect to the future did not come off; and, as the time limit has expired, there is no possibility of their subsequent fulfilment.

Cheiro knew me as he sat peering over my hand, and was well acquainted with my psychological work; and it was not difficult for him to particularise in certain instances with some certainty, as well as indulge in those more or less vague generalisations which, by a little stretch here and a repression or gliding-over there, can be made to fit in with most people's past, present, and future.

I quite frankly told Cheiro that I did not believe in palm-reading as a means of arriving at the unknown, and that the lines of the hand afforded no more indication of what was hidden from the ordinary eye than those of the left big toe or the sole of the right foot.

His semi-scientific exposition *in re* the palm, with its lines of Life and Death, Love and Hate, Good Fortune and Ill Fortune, and so forth, was quite good patter, and the sort of thing that would go down well with the impressionable ; but, alas ! it did not impress me. But the seer's method of fishing for points, his clear reading of facial expression and interpretation of physical indications, made no little impression upon me.

He was a shrewd reader of character ; and an intimate knowledge of human nature enabled him to arrive rapidly at conclusions with some outside accuracy. But where these outward readings ended there was no power of inside reading to carry him on, and he fell back upon vague conjecture and elastic generalities.

For Cheiro, the physiognomist and astute *homme du monde*, was no clairvoyant. In his heart he knew this as well as I myself did. But it was his profession to pose and assume. And, truth to tell, he did the posing and assuming remarkably well. He succeeded in impressing a considerable number of my friends, both before and subsequent to my investigation, with the fact that he was a most remarkable man with quite uncanny powers.

Amongst the bad shots Cheiro made in my case there was not one more wide of the mark than the assertion that I was both artistic and musical to a most gratifying extent. This, by the by, is an error into which most clairvoyants with whom I have come in contact seem to fall. For, as a matter of fact, I am not at all artistic ; my very best pavement effort would earn me the well-deserved contempt of the least critical daub-swallower that ever compassionately threw a penny in the curbstone hat. And my musical attainments are limited to the extent of barely being able to distinguish the difference between Beethoven in B and Yankee-Doodle.

Cheiro loved to invest his engaging personality with an air of mystery, which went well with the more impressionable section of an extensive *clientèle* who hung upon his utterances. He was half a Greek, half an Oriental, and of noble birth to boot. Like the king of mystics, Cagliostro, who, according to his story, had his origin somewhere where the East and the West meet, Cheiro sought to convey the impression that, whilst having imbibed the occultism of the East with his mother's milk, he had in later years acquired a knowledge of the more up-to-date mysticisms of the West. His linguistic gifts were considerable, and evidently he had read a good deal ; but his readings of human nature were, I am of opinion, more extensive and comprehensive than

his book-learning.   But what his fishing queries
did not elicit or his character-reading obtain was
filled in with information collected by outside
confederates with knowledge of the affairs and
inside history of the clients consulting him.

Whilst in London, Cheiro, so far as I am aware,
did not dabble in spiritualism.   The palm-reading,
clairvoyant art was enough for him.   It brought
him all the money plus the feminine favours he
required.   And then, in the heyday of his fame
there was not, as there is to-day, a spiritistic
boom on.

To-day, with its rush of sign-seekers anxious
for anything that will tickle the emotions, Cheiro,
subject to non-intervention on the part of the
police, would have become a most fashionable
and successful medium.

It was, I believe, chiefly owing to police inquiries that Cheiro thought it advisable to leave
London and take up his residence in Paris.   There
he speedily made a big success.   As a clairvoyant
mystic and man of the world he was quite the
vogue in good society in the French capital.   The
much-talked-of seeress, Madame de Thèbes, it is
understood, was a pupil of his.   Cheiro, who was
after money as well as *kudos*, saw in his popularity
his chances, and he made the most of them.
He became a financier, and his clients greedily
swallowed the scrip he caused to be manu-
factured.   As a financier, the Count—for he
found the assumption of a title useful in the realms
of finance—became quite a personage.   Who,
with his wonderful clairvoyant gifts, should know

what was what in things financial like this seer adviser ? Who indeed ? But the heaven-sent clairvoyant carried the financial pitcher once too often to the well of credulity. It fell ; and down with a crash came the financial house of cards, erected on bucket-shop lines. What the Count saved from the wreckage I do not know ; but it goes without saying there was very little left for those who had been induced to part with their savings under his inspiration and guidance.

I have lost sight of Cheiro for some time. The last time I saw him prosperity had caused him to put on flesh ; and a too plump seer is not so attractive to the feminine eye as one who retains slimmer proportions. The financial adversity through which he has passed since that occasion may have caused him to lose some of that superfluous flesh, which did not add to his personal attractiveness, and can hardly have increased his clairvoyant powers.

.   .   .   .   .

One of the most effective bits of clairvoyant fake, from the out-and-out fake point of view, I have yet encountered was demonstrated on shipboard by an American passenger, who, in the rôle of an amateur, also was out alike for money-making and *kudos*.

His *spécialité* was in telling from the backs thereof the colour of cards held up at some distance from where he stood.

His success was immediate, and, except in such instances where he pretended failure in order to add to the prevailing excitement and increase the amount wagered on the event, he never once made a mistake.

This feat he could do with a new pack of cards with the outward cover intact, directly obtained from the bar-tender, who was not in league with him.

The employment of this new "deck" did not impress me as it impressed others, as I was convinced that his readings were not made of the cards contained in the unbroken packet obtained from the bar-tender, but that, as in the case of Dr Slade and his slate, it was exchanged for another pack seemingly intact, which he had already manipulated for the purpose of the demonstration.

But how were the cards so manipulated that he could so readily distinguish them, with such unfailing accuracy ? It, I confess, puzzled me exceedingly, and the comments of the amateur seer were not exactly gratifying to my *amour propre*. The more I thought it over the more puzzled I became. On retiring to my cabin I closely, but vainly, studied pack after pack of cards in the desire to arrive at a solution.

Then as I lay in my bed musing over the various illustrations of the mystic I had witnessed during my travels and investigations, my thoughts went back to an Indian seer, who had done wonderful things in the clairvoyant reading line, particularly in the matter of cards. His success, I had determined, was due to the correct interpretation of apparently meaningless points of reflection.

But how could reflection be applied as a

solution to this fake? There was no mirror to be manipulated, as in the case of the Kattywar seer. In this case it was all plain sailing. You simply held up the back of the card, and he answered "black" or "red," as the case might be, without a moment's hesitation. He apparently had nothing to guide him beyond his eye, and what was unreadable to the ordinary eye was perfectly clear to his. He could not see the face of the card, as the colour did not show through, and it was by observing the backs that he arrived at his conclusions.

What was on those card backs? How were they so faked as to become so unhesitatingly readable?

Eureka! I was out of bed in a second. Up went the electric light, and a fresh pack of cards was in my hands. I carefully separated the black from the red, and made two decks of them —one black, one red. Then squeezing the former tightly together, I ran a sharp knife up each side of them. This, I felt, would denote the difference beween the two sets of cards when held up in the light. I commenced testing my theory, and found that the shimmering edges of the cards I had scraped were clearly defined in the light. Again and again I made the test, so that I could with the greatest ease distinguish the black from the red, for the latter, being unscraped, showed up smooth in the light, minus the shimmering edges appertaining to the black cards.

I took my knowledge with me to the smoking-room that evening and awaited developments.

The amateur seer was particularly sarcastic in his comments upon my inability to discover how the oracle was worked.

"Decided to give it best?" he went on, with a self-satisfied smile.

"As you like," I replied. "But it does seem odd that what is apparently so simple to you should be a matter of impossibility with everyone else."

"Why don't you have a try? You never know your luck. It might come to you as readily as it comes to me. Say, you stand here and have a shot at what I hold up."

I agreed.

He held up a card; but I, of course, was unaware which suite he had "readied" for the occasion, so my first declaration would have to be based purely upon guesswork.

The edges of the card held up were frayed, but whether a black or a red, there was at that moment nothing to indicate.

"I'll bet you a dollar you don't call it correctly first shot."

I nodded, and called out "Red."

"Well, it happens to be black, and you are out a dollar. Have another try."

I assented, and he held up another card. That had not been scraped.

"Oh, that," I said, with an air of firm conviction, "is another black."

"Wrong again; for this time it happens to be a red, and you are out two dollars. Shall we have another dollar on this?"

"Make it five."

" Five it is ; and the colour is—— ? "

" Red."

" And red is correct, and I owe you three dollars. Shall we make it six, or nothing ? "

" Yes ; and the card you now hold is another red."

" And that makes it nothing, for this particular card happens to be a black. Shall we have five on the next ? "

I nodded, and correctly described the next card, and the next, being thus a winner of ten dollars.

" A final one for twenty," he said, selecting a card from the pack he held.

That I too correctly designated.

The seer so far had not arrived at the knowledge that I was aware of the manner in which the oracle was worked, and put my conclusions down to mere chance guesses accompanied by luck.

" Bit lucky, aren't you ? " he asked. " Well, let's try your luck for something worth trying for. I will lay you fifty dollars you don't correctly guess the colour of the next half-dozen cards I hold up." The man was a sport.

Being quite sure of my ground, I accepted the wager, and won the fifty dollars, which the seer paid up, together with what had gone before, with quite good spirit.

" Say," said he afterwards, " how did you tumble on to it ? I thought I was quite safe. You won't give the show away whilst on board, or I shan't have any money or reputation left by the time I land."

I did not give the show away, as the seer,

whilst doing no harm, had succeeded in tickling people's interest and curiosity to an extent out of the common. As a professional medium or clairvoyant he might well have been a real danger, as he had a sleight-of-hand knowledge beyond the ordinary, and a plausibility that the most conscienceless professional mystic might well have envied.

I fancy most of the folk on board the boat were convinced that this dapper young American not only had genuine clairvoyant powers, but that it was a pity he did not devote his time to developing these powers in order to follow the art professionally.

.   .   .   .   .   .

Another so-called clairvoyant, whom I met in the East, was also an American, although claiming relationship with a goodly number of the British aristocracy. He did not go in for showy fakes, or do little tricks that might readily be found out. His clairvoyant flight was of a much higher order. He specialised in locating hidden treasure and lost jewels; and, in his capacity as a seer, was a *persona grata* at more than one native Indian Court. I believe some money and a fair quantity of jewels were recovered under his auspices; but these finds, one may safely say, were due more to human assistance than to clairvoyance. He posed as a traveller of means, and, when he was in funds, he certainly did things *en prince*. For due monetary consideration it was not difficult to get native hirelings to secrete jewels for him to find. Before leaving India he had collected some valuable stones, the real ownership of which no one exactly knew, maybe not even the collector himself. He was well received at somewhat exclusive Residences and Agencies, and one most particular Governor of a Province found him both acceptable and entertaining. His collection of jewels, with the tales of origin and adventure his fancy invented, was everywhere admired. Towards the end whispers got around, and inquiries were being made as to his *bona fides*, both as a clairvoyant and traveller of means. When asked my opinion of him and his powers, my reply invariably called forth the remark that I was prejudiced. I was not prejudiced ; but the man from the first made a distinctly unfavourable impression upon me, although he certainly did his best to make himself agreeable to me. I read him for what he was—an ingenious pretender.

He got safely away from the East by giving an expensive banquet at Colombo to which everybody who was anybody was invited. But the host himself did not attend that banquet. By the hour of its commencement he was well on his way back to the States ; and thus he went out of the life of those who once had made much of him.

With the exit of this dabbler in the clairvoyant art I close my chapter on the claims and chicaneries of clairvoyance.

CHAPTER VI

SPIRIT PHOTOGRAPHY

HAVE I ever photographed a spirit? No!

Have I ever seen a spirit photographed? No!

Do I believe a *bona fide* spirit ever has been photographed? No! And yet there are those who claim to have photographed spirits, and others who have brought themselves to believe that they have had in their possession photographic presentments of visitors from the other world.

With such folk argument is futile. They prefer to believe and disdain to examine. Critical examination would but serve to upset their belief, and this is about the last thing they desire.

Just as people have been known to cling to spurious banknotes, with the pious hope that one day they may be realised at their face value, so do the unreasoning faithful cling to their equally spurious spirit counterfeits, with the belief that they are genuine and must eventually be accepted as good tender.

Nothing could be more convincing than a *bona fide* photograph of a spirit in proving existence in that other world as pictured by the believers in modern spiritism and the power of the spirit existence to manifest itself in this.

But where is the proof that such photographs have been taken ? Mere assertion is not proof. Belief, no matter how earnestly held and fervently expressed, in the absence of outside proof fails to carry with it conviction. It is not enough to confirm the belief of those who are already believers, or to provide conviction for those who wish only to believe without due examination.

I have seen what purported to be photographs of visitors from the other world ; but, in the absence of direct evidence as to how and when the visitation was made, and how and when what was claimed to be a genuine photo of such visitation was taken, I have always reserved to myself the right of having my doubts.

The first " spirit photo " I had the privilege of seeing was one of an Indian brave named Skiwaukee. The spirit form of this Indian was a feature at a séance which he honoured with his presence, and, as became a Redskin of renown in earth life, his spirit manifestations belonged to the " powerful " order of physical phenomena. Whilst the old Adam scalping instinct, it was given out, was not altogether dead within him, there is, I understand, no record of his having scalped any one of the admiring sitters during his visitations, although self-sacrifice on the part of the more spiritually exalted amongst the faithful would possibly have freely permitted such a catastrophe. For how could the momentary earthly pain of a ravished scalp-lock weigh with the sublime proof of spiritual power contained in the conveyance to that celestial wigwam in

the other world of this mundane trophy com-
memorating his visit to this mundane sphere of
his previous existence ?   And, again, what direct
evidence of this visit the hairless scalp of the shorn
one would disclose !   Unanswerable, quite !

I have had a fairly wide acquaintance with
Red Indians ; and when I was writing my book,
The Queen's Highway from Ocean to Ocean, describing Canada from the Pacific to the Atlantic, I
pitched my tent for a while with them out west ;
but outside of the Six Nations' chief I had never
come across such a perfect picture-book brave as
the spirit photo represented Skiwaukee to be.

I had a grave suspicion that the photo was
that of one of Buffalo Bill's " Wild West " braves
taken previously to his retirement from the earthly
show business.   Whilst the brave thus depicted
for spiritual conviction made, I must confess,
quite an attractive spirit photo, the make-up
was distinctly earthly, and the whole thing was
earmarked with photographic fake.

I knew Buffalo Bill well, and I mentioned
my suspicions to him.

With that sunny, big-hearted laugh of his, he
said : " Skiwaukee ! he wasn't one of my outfit.
Possibly he went to the Happy Hunting-grounds
before I took the road.   But, for fake purposes,
any name's as good as another for an Injin.   I
would have liked to have had a sittin' with this
Skiwaukee.   I guess I'd 've put him through his
pacings."   I guess he would, and that it would
not have been an altogether pleasant experience
for the manifesting brave.

Buffalo Bill had no great faith in a Redskin's translation to a celestial sphere, but guessed that when they passed in their " earthly checks " they were done with, and that, even allowing their celestial translation, they would be too much occupied in chasing buffalo shades in Shadowland to be at the beck and call of any dollar-snatching medium who might fancy he had a " rake-off " on a séance manifestation.

" Red Shirt," that prominent chief of the Wild West show, might well have sat for the spirit-portrait of the departed " Skiwaukee." But this brave in real life was too much of a handful to contemplate as a spirit manifesting amongst the scalpable at a dark séance.

I once had an interesting experience with him at a luncheon at the Welcome Club at the Earl's Court Exhibition. I was asked to read his thoughts. I made the attempt. The first thing he did was to think of a carving-knife lying on the table ; and the next for me to draw it across the throat of the manager, with whom, through some fancied grievance, he was seriously disgruntled. Obviously I did not allow him to give effect to this method of wiping out old scores. Then his thoughts centred upon a beautiful and stately duchess sitting at the end of the table. To her I went, and passed my left hand over her perfectly-coiffured head. There was a tremulous eagerness in his right hand grasping the knife. The dominant idea in his mind at the moment was to relieve her of her hair. But actual scalping has not yet been included in my illustrations of reading unuttered thought.   It was sufficient to anticipate the desire and to prevent its accomplishment.   But in passing my hand over the fair victim's hair a piece of transformation came away; and whilst this act seemed to give a mollified sort of satisfaction to my " subject," the look the dear duchess gave me did not convey an equal satisfaction, although she graciously murmured " Wonderful ! " when she was informed that Red Shirt had had her in his mind and no one else.

A photo of a spirit Indian in the act of scalping a mortal, to me at least, would be more interesting and convincing than that of one merely posing to make a pretty picture.

Other " spirit photos " I have seen since my first introduction to spirit photography have been more shadowy and less clearly defined than that depicting Skiwaukee; but, to my mind, they have been just as much a fake.   The fake art is not unknown in photography, and a skilful photographer, unburdened with scruples, would experience little difficulty in producing fake spirit photos; and, given a portrait of the one whose spirit form was to be produced to work on, an acceptable likeness of a shadowy character might very well be arrived at.

" But," will answer the out-and-out believer, who is unable to question and who finds conviction in blind acceptance alone, " what about the photos of spirits taken by members of the family, to whom alone they have directly appeared ? "

Yes, indeed, what about them ?   What independent witness saw the appearance and saw the photo taken, and had his eye and hand on the plate up to the close of its development ?

In response to my public inquiries for proofs of spirit identity, the nearest approach in the shape of evidence in connection with spirit photography has been the offer to show me photos which are alleged to have been taken of appearances made within the knowledge of those who possess the exhibits. This is not the form of evidence that would bring with it the conviction I am in search of.

Sir Arthur Conan Doyle, I gather, claims to possess evidence of spirit appearances which have provided material for photographic reproduction. But my earnestly expressed desire in a recent letter in the *Daily Express* (which virile paper, as one may well imagine, has, in connection with the craze, been on the side of sanity and common sense) for a convincing manifestation of this description remains unsatisfied.

Am I never to see a spirit that can be photographed, or a snapshot taken of such a palpable visitation ?

Next to the impossible wish of myself seeing her and getting her photograph under my personal observation, there is one spirit of whom I would like to possess a really authentic photograph. I refer to the White Lady of Potsdam. She is the wraith, the banshee, of the House of Hohenzollern; and her appearance denotes a dire fatality to the head of that august family.

This lady of woe has not, I understand, put in an appearance since the Emperor William I. was called to his fathers.   I was in Morocco at that time, and consequently was unable to personally investigate the claims then current as to her visitation.

As a visitor from the other world this White Lady would have special interest for me.   I have successfully read the thoughts of two German Emperors, and other shining lights of the House of Hohenzollern ; and this has made me long for the opportunity of reading the mind of that dead spirit, whose earthly visits are associated with such portentous happenings.   I would like to get at first hand who she really is, what ails her, and why she is forced or impelled to return to earth as a messenger of woe.

The Kaiser, although with but little leaning towards supernaturalism, is not, I believe, altogether superior to the generally accepted superstition respecting this family ghost ; and the mere rumour that she was said to have been seen on the occasion of his visit to Vienna in connection with the funeral of the Emperor Francis Joseph was, I am informed, sufficient to cause him to hurriedly leave the Austrian capital, where, amidst the prevailing political unrest, his life was thought to be in some danger.

The Emperor Carl's little weakness in the matter of superstition includes a belief in omens ; and he, I understand, conveyed his forebodings and fears to the Kaiser, who deemed it advisable to return, with scant ceremony, to Berlin, to the satisfaction of the mystically inclined mother of the Emperor, at whose mystic belief it has frequently pleased the Kaiser Wilhelm to poke fun. I would say that, with the grip she has upon her somewhat nerveless son, the Empress-mother is to-day the real ruler of Austria.

When I experimented with the old Kaiser William he had in his mind the figures 1861, and I wrote on a blackboard '61, which represented the year of his coronation as King of Prussia. As his Majesty afterwards said, "What else should I think of? That is uppermost in my thoughts."

The present Kaiser gave me the impression that '71 and the Versailles event would have been a more fitting thought on the part of his august grandfather, and, curiously enough, there ran through his mind at that moment the figures 1917. They had no significance for me at that time; but subsequent events have caused me to wonder if premonition gave birth to this passing thought, and with what this premonition might be associated.

For a time I wondered if the White Lady would elect to put in an appearance during the year 1917, foreshadowing an immediate or early event of world-wide moment. But the year 1917 has run its course, and so far there is no sign of the White Lady. It may have been that the figures 1917, forming the Kaiser's thoughts, may have been based upon some event as yet undisclosed, or he may have anticipated something by a year or so.

When, however, the White Lady does appear, I trust occasion will be taken to photograph her. It is one that should not be missed.

I will gladly pay £100 for an authentic spirit photograph of this lady, preferably for one bearing her autograph in her own spirit handwriting.

Such an offer does not, I take it, come within the regulations bearing upon trading with the enemy ; but the snapshot of the "other-world" visitor could be taken by a neutral possessing spirit-seeing gifts, and the attestation of any two of the representatives of the neutral Powers still resident in the Prussian capital as to the genuineness of the production would satisfy me.

CHAPTER VII

ALL the trance mediums I have seen have been exceedingly good actors, with quite an abnormal gift of the gab. Whilst " under the influence " they have been ready to talk upon any subject ; but not one has ever told me anything worth knowing, no matter by what spirit he or she was for the time-being controlled. When the controlling spirit has been that of some at one time ordinary mortal desirous of communicating with this world, too high expectations of the intelligence conveyed through the mouth of the medium would have been unreasonable. But when the spirits of the classic dead are roped in to utter meaningless drivel that could have had no place in their thoughts when on earth, the effect produced upon any sitter, beyond those ready and willing to swallow anything in the shape of " spirit communications," is one of sheer disgust. Admitting—a proposition to me quite impossible of acceptance—that it is indeed the spirit of some-one once great on earth who speaks, the sad fact is brought strikingly home to one of the mental deterioration that takes place on translation to the spiritual sphere. And, judging by what I have heard, the longer the residence in the other world, the greater the deterioration.

It is monstrous that the spirits of the classic dead should be roped in in this fashion just to provide unscrupulous mediums with dollars, and the sign-seekers forming the audience with "convincing evidence." But one may rest assured that the spirits who are alleged to control the mediums have no part whatever in the sorry entertainment. The voice is that of the medium, as are the uttered thoughts. According to the knowledge and education of the officiating medium, so do the illuminating spirit utterances shape themselves.

To hear the medium, whilst under this alleged control, change his or her voice to fit in with the rôle assumed is more diverting than convincing ; and the physical emotion displayed by the medium is no evidence whatever that it emanates from the invisible controlling spirit.

When I have seen that rolling of the medium's eyes, that twitching of the mouth, wringing of the hands, and other physical contortions, I have invariably arrived at the conclusion that the spirit's lot could not have been a particularly happy one, and that it was unkind in the extreme to get him to "manifest" under such distressing conditions.

In a lunatic asylum one expects exhibitions of this kind with patients who have worked themselves into the belief that they are possessed by devils or some such disturbing influence. One humours these poor creatures, and takes precautions that they do themselves no personal injury. But in professional spiritualism, seemingly sane sitters find in the ecstatic raptures or facial contortions of the medium direct evidence not only of spirit presence, but of the mental and physical condition of the spirit prevailing at that moment. And they gladly pay for the privilege of being fooled.

Now and again it may happen that an extra neurotic medium may work herself up to believe that she is really mediumistic, and the rest follows. To the extent of this self-assumption the possession is genuine ; but the possession is no more spiritual than that which begets similar demonstrations on the part of obsessed inmates of an insane asylum. But professional mediums, as a rule, are free from this phase of self-deception. They are out to deceive and to make a position and money out of the deception. It is just a bit of acting, overdone mostly, but here and there with little touches that are quite artistic. But the artistic side, considering the grave character of the demonstration, is lost sight of in the pretence and fraud knowingly practised.

An unexpected pin-prick, if it be deep enough, will straightway cause the medium to throw off his or her trance, thus emphasising the superficial hold the spirit influence has upon the medium. At the risk of inflicting pain upon the controlling spirit, I have been a party to this surely permissible physical test. In not one instance within my remembrance has the spirit, who had addressed us with such volubility through the officiating trance medium, received—so far at least as one could discover—the faintest scratch ; although it has brought his visitation to an abrupt close.

One is always warned at such séances not to disturb the medium for fear of inconveniencing the spirit.   Spirits are exceedingly touchy sort of folk, and, whilst their disembodied selves are inside the human envelope provided by the presiding medium, resent any mundane interference with this sympathetic human covering.

These visitors from the other world resent also anything approaching even the mildest of hecklings.   I must confess to having heckled more than one manifesting spirit when, as it were, I found him " talking through his hat." True believers have found me in this " most unreasonable."   The crime of my unreasonableness has consisted in putting little posers which the spirit has been either unable or disinclined to answer.   On several occasions he has retired hurriedly in a tiff, and the medium in a corresponding tiffish mood has declared the manifestation over.

Foreign spirits, affecting a language assumedly foreign to the medium whom they have chosen as their earthly mouthpiece, get their rags out with distinctly human quickness when those who know their tongue take exception to the grammatical correctness or otherwise of the subject-matter of their discourse.

" Dear things ! " I have heard feminine believers consolingly say by way of explanation ; " they have been so long absent from earth that one can understand them forgetting their own language. There is nothing so easy to forget as a language one has no occasion to speak in " ; which goes to say that foreign spirits drop their mother tongue when they pass over the Border, unless, when they elect to reappear in this form of visitation, they speak through a medium who is conversant with the tongue in which they would be expected to speak. Language efficiency on the part of the medium makes for correctness on the part of the spirit, just as inefficiency leads to incorrectness and difficulty in the matter of response.

There are those, however, who aver they have been the recipients of most extraordinary information through mediums who were not of the professional class. These gifted beings were in every way above suspicion, and the trance condition into which they were thrown, whilst under spiritual influence, was wholly unsought by them. Some of these gifted folk have been the channel chosen for the most illuminating " communications," of which they themselves could not possibly have had the faintest personal knowledge. And again, they have spoken in tongues entirely foreign to them.

But beyond the mere statement that it was as related, there was furnished no evidence in confirmation of the statement, and it is just this independent confirmatory evidence that is wanted, and that invariably is lacking. So long as people in private life like being deceived and are blind to their own self-deception, so long shall we hear of mystic wonders being performed in the family circle, the truth and honesty associated with which are beyond question.

And though such people profess to have greater faith in the spiritistic illustrations emanating from their own mediumistic friends and relations than in those coming through professional mediums, they seldom fail to give the professionals their support ; indeed, it would be difficult to see how those adopting spiritualism as a money-making concern could thrive without them. This support they have accorded to professionals of exceedingly shady reputation, of whom not a few have eventually met with well-merited exposure. My memory goes back to two trance mediums who were much in favour amongst the elect in the earlier days of the movement. They in the end came to grief ; but before exposure overtook them they collected a big following and much money. Fletcher was their name, and they hailed from America. They gave public discourses on Sundays ; and it was considered quite the correct thing in the spiritualistic world to attend them. I sat at the feet of the Fletchers, and I was not enlightened by what I saw or heard. The man was an obsequious creature with the appearance of a mute. His get-up was most funereal, and his mock solemnity, attuned to suit the tastes of his sign-seeking followers, to a simple inquirer like myself was positively oppressive.

Like other professional mediums, they carried the leaky pitcher of imposture once too often to the well of credulity. A duped follower kicked, and a prosecution followed. Mrs Fletcher was found guilty, and the career of the Fletcher couple as professional mediums, so far at least as this country was concerned, was ended.

But they still found sympathisers and believers who maintained that the conviction was unjustly obtained and that the prosecutrix had displayed a vindictiveness that was most reprehensible. What was the loss of money compared with the injury to the medium's health and consequent loss of her spiritistic powers ? Money could be replaced ; but mediumistic power, once destroyed, was lost for ever. No great loss to the world, truly !

A pretty argument, I will admit. But the " dear spirits " should not go out of their way to enrich the mediums through whom they elect to manifest ; and to drag in the dear spirits in order to cajole money out of dupes is, I take it, an uncommonly low-down thing.

There is, however, generally money somewhere in the case when a medium is caught breaking the law of the land.

It was also so with that specious seeress, " The Swami," and her degraded husband, Jackson. They mouthed about the occult and impressed the ignorant with their claims to miraculous powers ; at the same time, however, they were out for making all they could, not overlooking even the scullery-maid's hoarded savings. The trial of these low-down charlatans disclosed a scandalous state of affairs : trickery of the lowest type, immorality of the grossest. And

9

yet before the exposure came " The Swami " was looked upon by a certain section of the credulous as little short of " heaven-sent "; and that co-partner of hers in chicanery and immorality was said to have gifts that were as spiritual as they were miraculous—and they were neither.

The term of imprisonment they underwent for their crime, considering the extent and character of their offences against society, did not err on the side of severity. This world has no use for such depraved impostors, whatever the next may have to say on the matter.

I do not see, moreover, what use this world has for any professional trance mediums of any type.

.   .   .   .   .

Of all the phases of spirit phenomena, that of spirit writing, under the conditions in which it is produced, is the most unsatisfactory and inconclusive. It also lends itself readily to self-deception and chicanery.

" I feel myself controlled," says the medium, having convinced himself that he is mediumistic, " and I write at the dictation of my control."

Good ! But wherein lies the proof that spirit influence has any connection whatever with the scribbled sentences that the writer puts down with *his own hand* ? The writing may vary from his own handwriting and take a form approaching as near as possible that which he has worked himself up to believe the spirit itself might adopt. But the writing and the text of the message, whatever form assumed, come through *his own hand*.

It is not enough to say that he feels himself controlled, and that his hand, whilst "under this influence," takes a part unconscious of its own volition. Something more than this is needed to establish a proof that the writing is the outcome of spirit power.

When that visitor from the other world manifested at Belshazzar's feast, the hand was clearly visible to the awestricken king and his carousing guests as it traced its message in letters of flame upon the wall. It remained there long enough for all to read and for Daniel to interpret it.

Now, it is up to celestial visitors of to-day to show their own hand in writing messages such as they are able to convey to an expectant world ; and if it should happen that the message so written is unintelligible to those favoured with the communication, then it might remain in evidence until someone able to correctly decipher and interpret it could be brought to the scene. But any hand, great or small, any writing in any language momentarily readable or otherwise—no jugglery being possible—would in itself constitute a proof of spirit visitation.

To this the only-too-ready-to-believe-anything spiritist will doubtless retort : " Is it not enough to have such a message come through the hand of one in whom I have implicit confidence ? Is it not enough for the message to come through my own hand, written with my own pencil or upon my own typewriter ? "

No, it is not enough.

It may satisfy your out-and-out believer, but

it fails to satisfy me. And in this there are, I hope, others who will think with me.

Let the spirit signify its presence and its desire to make a written communication by taking up a pen or pencil in its own hand, and not operate through that of a mere human who may claim to feel the influence of the presence. Let the spirit manipulate the typewriter itself, wholly independent of human manipulation thereof.

If, as it may be pleaded, the spirit may be ignorant of the working of a typewriting machine, then, in the absence of a training-school in the other-world of modern spiritism where the visitor in the interval of his earthly visits could acquire a knowledge of the typewriting art, lay on a spirit who on earth life had mastered a typewriter. For the purposes of such a convincing proof this little matter might well be arranged.

It is just this convincing proof, however, that the votaries of spiritism seem most reluctant to furnish. To convince themselves and those who think with them is apparently all-sufficient, and so we get no "forrarder."

The mania for giving expression to messages from the other world is, I am inclined to think, strongest with those with a natural itch for scribbling. With them it is so easy to dash off messages and label them spiritual ; and it is not difficult for them to convince themselves that the writing was actually the outcome of spirit control and not the result of their own mental vagaries.

I have seen writers, whilst under the belief that they have been spirit-controlled, scribble for dear life on sheets of paper in front of them, trying to look and to feel parts appropriate to the spirit in control. The phase of mentality of the spirit writer is precisely on all-fours with that of the trance medium. Only, the one lets off spiritual steam with his hand and the other with his mouth ; and under the circumstances in which these other-world manifestations are presented, there is nothing tangible or convincing about them.

And, amongst these writing mediums, there are undoubtedly those who have no part to play in the alluring game of deception : men who honestly believe in the existence of a spirit control and in the accuracy of their statements associated therewith.

Such a man was Mr W. T. Stead. He was a perfervid, emotional man, but absolutely honest. He had his own way of thinking things out and of carrying them out, but any conclusions he might arrive at were honestly formed and fearlessly held. Whilst it was always easy to admire his ability and feel some of his enthusiasm, it at times was exceedingly difficult to see eye to eye with him in his reasonings and accept his conclusions.

The latter-day conclusions in connection with so-called spirit phenomena at which he arrived were, obviously, not within my acceptance. We had many talks over the occult ; and, whilst I found him ever anxious to probe mysteries and get at the bottom of things generally, he showed no distinct tendency towards accepting, as being of mundane origin, occurrences which had no better basis for acceptance as supernatural than that they had been labelled as such.

He had, however, a highly impressionable temperament, and, the chord of belief once touched, there was no knowing to what extent he might bring himself to believe.

The last time I saw him was at his office off the Embankment. He had asked me to meet a queer " card " who had travelled a little and, in my opinion, assumed far too much.

Amongst these assumptions was the claim that he could tell the height, weight, character, and thoughts of a man by merely studying his footprint from behind.

This assumption apparently impressed Stead, and he was pleased to say that his visitor had got ahead of me in divining thought from a footprint. Indeed he had.

Another claim of this unconvincing Yankee was that he had mastered monkey language to the extent not only of understanding it, but of being able to converse in it. For the purpose of pursuing his investigations and carrying on conversations with these jabberers of the jungle he had had a cage constructed which was set up in places most frequented by them. The spectacle of the learned professor squatting in the cage carrying on an argument with various missing-link species must have been singularly instructive and not a little humorous. The humorous aspect of the situation was the one most to impress me. But the professor was intensely serious over it all, and the reason, maybe, why he somewhat resented my mental attitude on the subject was that he was devoid of the saving sense of humour.

The question of monkey language interested me exceedingly, and I explained to Mr Stead and his friend the naturalist how my special interest therein arose.

At a durbar at Bhavanagar a learned pundit had composed some yards of learned twaddle chiefly bearing upon myself, which he read at length to the native prince and his *entourage*, apparently to their edification and interest.

Two gems stood out in association with this lengthy oration. One was that it was established beyond question that the gods had bestowed upon me the power to read the human mind and know the human character, but this power did not extend to reading that of the monkey. Neither did it permit of my restoring to them their lost language. It was explained that at one time the monkeys had an intelligible language ; but for an offence against the gods, that was taken from them, and, until the gods should choose to take off the ban, the animals, for all understandable purposes, would remain as they were.

It was most kind of the gods to endow me as it was alleged they were good enough to have done ; but I am glad they did not increase their gifts to the extent of restoring to the monkeys their lost tongue.

Now, if it should happen that the monkey

recovers his speech, what known language, think you, would it most resemble ?

I have arrived at a fairly definite idea on the matter ; but as the people whom I have in mind might resent my conclusions, I shall keep them to myself. It, however, is open to anyone to mentally speculate on the point.

That the power to read monkey-mind was withheld from me by the gods is, I would say, slightly inaccurate.

I have read the thoughts of a monkey, and a remarkably easy experiment it was.

He had hidden an orange, after fooling about with it, as is a monkey's way, and I took him as a subject. It was a thousand to one that his entire thought for the moment would be concentrated upon the hidden fruit. It was, and I at once went to the place where it lay *perdu*. That was sufficient for my test ; but the monkey was not out for satisfying me, but himself, and when I stooped to annex my find he promptly annexed my hand with his teeth. Failing to convey a verbal understanding to my jabbering subject, I administered a physical one, which sent him flying across the room.

I have often wondered whether monkeys in the primordial, missing-link, or latter-day stage find translations to that other world so freely drawn upon by professing mediums ; for some of the manifestations I have witnessed have been of the most monkeyish description, and such as the spirit of no self-respecting human would ever demean himself by demonstrating.

I did not put this point to the American ; but had I done so, I feel pretty confident that all his peculiar and exclusive knowledge of monkeys and monkey-land would not have enabled him to reply to it with any degree of certainty.

I think one may date Mr Stead's first leanings towards the supernatural from coming under the influence of this exceedingly plausible person. Then came further beliefs and temperamental questionings, and the final obsession—Julia.

CHAPTER VIII

SUBJECTIVE VISIONS AND FALSE SENSORIAL IMPRESSIONS

THE common error with spiritualistic devotees is to mistake purely subjective for objective phenomena. "I know what I have seen," will say the vision-seer, "and nothing will convince me that it was a mere hallucination." Nothing, I fear, outside of an earthquake will convince folk who argue from this standpoint. The vision they affect to have seen is, with them, as actual as a fleeting neuralgic pain. There is no need to question their veracity on this point ; it is their inability to properly weigh and adjust matters which is at fault. They see what they aver they have seen, all right, but probably neither at the time nor on the occasion fixed for the occurrence, and then certainly never more than in the mind's eye.

In a word, the vision is of the subjective and not, as they assume, of the objective order of spirit phenomena.

This seeing of visions is quite a common occurrence with those who are out to receive proofs of that visible life Beyond in accordance with their anticipations and desire. I have received many letters on this subject from people undoubtedly sincere in their convictions. These visions, they go on to say, have been the direct outcome of their own observation and not through a medium. Where, therefore, they ask, does trickery come in?

Although, in the first instance, the medium has no direct part in the accepted visitation, trickery of a kind does come in, all the same. It is the senses which are tricked. And later on, maybe, when the vision-seer, seeking for a further sign and additional proof, has recourse to a medium for that purpose, nine times out of ten he will be tricked with intent. But as he is only looking for confirmation, he finds it in any far-fetched assumption mediumistic ingenuity and plausibility may advance.

One of the most typical cases of the un-questioning acceptance of a purely subjective as distinct from an objective vision, and how visits to mediums serve to confirm a longing that apparently was solely looking for confirmation irrespective of logical reasoning, and with a proneness to accept, without due examination, mere inferences from facts for facts themselves, is contained in a statement contributed to a recent number of the *London* magazine. My attention was called to this article on its publication by a valued literary friend of mine, who has given some thought to the subject of spirit-istic phenomena, asking for my views on the matter. These I briefly gave him, and he wrote saying that I had made quite clear what at first had been really difficult to understand.

At the same time the editor of *London* was good enough to ask me to write him an article on the subject. This I did ; but my views, which had made matters so clear to my inquiring friend, apparently collided with those already adopted by the editor. But, in view of the interest aroused in the statements published in *London*, I give in this chapter my reply thereto as written for publication in that popular magazine.

.   .   .   .   .   .

Mr Richard Wilkinson is not the only one whom the war has caused to think. It has brought with it, too, feelings and longings which previously can well be said to have had no conscious existence. Fathers, mothers, for the first time in their lives, have had all their thoughts and feelings centred upon their loved ones, facing danger and death away from their side. This in itself is sufficient to beget a condition of mental exaltation that permits of their seeing, hearing, and anticipating things that had had no previous being in their everyday lives. And after the arrival of that fateful War Office message, it is indeed hard for them to believe that this side of the grave there shall be no further communication with the young life thus suddenly cut off.

I am frequently asked by those who themselves claim to have had experiences of seemingly inexplicable phenomena, or who relate those said to have been experienced by people for whose good faith they can vouch, to explain these alleged occurrences.

They, in the majority of cases, have already satisfied themselves that the occurrences, being to them inexplicable, must perforce be of supernatural origin.

Now, in such matters the wisest course to pursue is to first exhaust the natural for an explanation before rushing to the supernatural to furnish a solution of what, from previous experience, seems to be inexplicable.

So, starting upon the hypothesis of the supernatural, what explanation would be satisfactory that did not materially accord with the already accepted theory of origin?

One is expected to agree and accept without criticism—which, frankly, I cannot—or furnish offhand, without data, an explanation, which in its turn would be ruled out as not being applicable to the particular phenomena in question.

Now, I ask, is it reasonable to expect a man, no matter what his experience has been or what attention he has devoted to the subject, to explain offhand the why and wherefore of alleged manifestations of which he himself has not been a witness, and of which admittedly there is very little, if any, really independent corroborating evidence?

Ordinary things in this world very seldom occur exactly as related. And when it comes to phenomena which cannot be weighed or measured by generally accepted standards, the relation, in the desire to impress the inexplicability thereof, does not as a rule err on the side of exactness. Little gaps are bridged over, and

times and dates are altered in order that the
narrative may span or fit in the better. All this
may be done in perfect good faith, and without
the slightest intention to exaggerate or deceive.
But the tendency to get things, which in reality
are allied neither in time nor in circumstance,
to run on all-fours with the dominating desire
of the seeker after the sign plays havoc with
memory, and causes the requisite detail and
sequence to be matters of but little moment.

Mr Wilkinson's narrative in the October issue
of *London* is plain and straightforward enough
to suit the most exacting critic. He evidently
writes direct from the heart and with full conviction. As he has given his experiences to the
public, and those to whom I have referred as
having communicated with me have not, I
will, at this stage, confine myself to dealing with
the occurrences he has made known to the readers
of this magazine.

By far the most striking of them, and the one
which in itself, if it were indeed a reality, would
furnish an unquestionable proof of spirit visitation, is the instance of the son's appearance after
death to his mother.

But consider the conditions under which the
appearance was made. Mrs Wilkinson was
nursing her dying father at Brighton, and in
the very nature of things her thoughts and
longings would go out to the son she unhappily
had but recently lost. It would not, therefore,
be difficult to conjure up a vision of him. That
Mrs Wilkinson believes she saw what her husband

states cannot of course be questioned for a single moment. And that she actually saw the form may also be admitted. But it, I take it, was of a subjective and not of an objective nature. It was in the mind's eye right enough, but no more. And had Mrs Wilkinson placed her hands over her eyes, she, according to my belief, would still have seen the form. Had there been no form in front of her, with her eyes thus covered, the inference would be that it was objective rather than merely suggestive. It is a simple test ; but those to whom such assumed visitations are desired would, I fancy, hesitate to shut out by the application of this test so welcome a vision for even so brief a space.

Years ago, whilst staying at Clopton Manor, near Stratford-on-Avon, I was located in a ghost-haunted room. The blood of the spirit—who on earth-life was a victim of the Civil War—still stained the anteroom leading off the bedroom. The spirit manifested by my bedside one night. But, prior to testing its substantiality by hurling a heavy silver candlestick at its head, I bethought myself of covering my eyes with my hands. The form was still there. I had heard much of this ghostly visitation during my stay at Clopton Manor ; and I would like to know if Joan had mentioned the fact of her having seen Roger " under conditions which placed out of bounds the possibility of its having been a dream " to Mrs Wilkinson *before* she herself had that vision of her son. The relation of such an experience, it goes without saying, would increase the inherent longing and expectancy which are all-important factors in the creation of subjective visitations.

That Mrs Wilkinson's letters were in Roger's sachet, is to say they were in the very place in which they might well be expected to be found ; and it is far more reasonable to assume that she had overlooked them than that spirit influence obtained through a medium, with whom she had previously been unacquainted, had indicated their whereabouts. As to the coin incident, one may assume that its existence had been forgotten. Subconsciousness has much to answer for in such matters. But it is apparently easier to give the credit to the supernatural than to discover a slip in the natural.

As to the " Edward " incident. The name of the fourth attendant spirit might well have been given by the medium as, say, Tom ; and in the family somewhere or other a departed one of that name might presumably have been found to fit in with the information. The second medium whom Mr Wilkinson consulted, although mentioning Elizabeth, John, and William, seemingly omits any mention of Edward. This is understandable, as Edward was but twelve weeks old when he departed this earth ; and, unless he had developed with extraordinary rapidity, it is difficult to understand how he could have been an attendant spirit on Roger on his entry into spiritland unless he were carried by Elizabeth, John, or William, who were already grown up.

Having had, as it appears to them, a slight

lifting of the veil giving an insight into the Beyond, it is but natural that receivers of these signs and portents should seek in every way possible for further signs and confirmation of the new belief that has sprung into existence. But any really direct communications are scarcely likely to be obtained through the agency of a medium, professional or otherwise.

It, I take it, should be clear to the most out-and-out believer that if a spirit be able to manifest, that manifestation would be made direct to those nearest and dearest to it in this world, and not through the mediumship of someone of whose existence or habitation it, on earth-life, would, presumably, have had no knowledge whatever. It, therefore, is unreasonable to assume that manifestations through such sources can be accepted as convincing realities. But with seekers after signs, plain, matter-of-fact reasonableness is invariably ignored. It is the sign or the further sign they want. That, with them, is all that matters.

And, whilst no further indication of spirit existence may come to them direct, the medium, having duly measured the longings and beliefs of the seekers, will invariably provide—for a monetary consideration or otherwise—the intelligence for which the inquirer is in search.

But it is not of mediums and their ways, of the chicaneries I have exposed, and the alleged " spirit forms " materialised at their séances I have unmasked, of which I will speak here. It is too long a story.

10

I confine myself to dealing with that higher phase of the belief in the supernatural which is closely associated with those who, although in my opinion self-deceived, really believe. But I repeat my warning about such real believers having recourse to mediums. In that way possible, and indeed probable, deception lies. Mediums of the unprofessional class, who hug the *kudos* associated in certain quarters with alleged mediumistic gifts, and those of the professional class, who are out to make all they can out of their opportunities, cannot very well be expected to be on the same spiritual plane as their inquirers, however much they may be willing to help or oblige them, according to their lights.

I must be excused if I question the accuracy of the statements, as a rule, made of the results obtained at such mediumistic consultations. To more properly judge of their value and relevancy one would need to be present at such consultations, to carefully observe the emotional indications which may be quite unconsciously conveyed by the inquirer to the medium, and to equally carefully note question and answer and other running verbal communications passing between them. In this way one would be able to form a more accurate opinion of how the medium arrived at his or her conclusions, and the consequent conveyance of information from Spiritland.

I lay particular stress upon this, as I notice there seems to be a fairly general opinion that the results may be the outcome of telepathy, the thoughts of the inquirer being unconsciously conveyed to the medium. As one who has given some study to the subject of thought-reading, and has put in practice the art or the gift, whichever you care to term it, with "subjects" of all nationalities, I must say that I cannot accept this theory as an explanation of the phenomena. Thought cannot be conveyed one to the other in this fashion. Thought itself is an immaterial quantity, and has no method of affording readable expression other than through the physical system. A look, a touch, a sigh, or any other emotional indication may tell much ; but beyond this, thought tells nothing that is really readable.

Just as the seekers after spirit-signs mistake inferences from facts for facts, so do those who affect to believe in psychic force mistake intuition for clairvoyance, and the intelligent interpretation of facial signs and other physical indications for readings of the mind itself. Through the body the mind can, and does, express itself, but that is not enough for the "psychic forcers." They prefer the brain-wave theory. It is so much more soul-satisfying, or "tony," as the Americans would say.

Mr Wilkinson concludes with the trite assertion that " no one of us has a monopoly of truth," adding, that by searching the beliefs of others we may find that which answers our greatest need.

To this, by way of conclusion, I would say, and no one of us can have a monopoly of these supernatural indications. If visitations from the other world indeed be possible, then, in the interests of truth—where such visitations would be a welcome and a consolation—let them be universal. In this way would the truth be brought home to those who are unable to accept as realities isolated instances, occurring in circumstances and under conditions of which they have no immediate knowledge.

.   .   .   .   .   .

Mr Arthur Machen, who, judging by his publicly expressed opinions on the subject, has not, apparently, quite made up his mind as to where we really are in connection with the so-called occult, but who, sensible man that he is, refuses to accept every wild-cat statement that comes along, is, I gather, inclined to the belief that thought transference may have played some part in connection with Mr Wilkinson's mediumistic experiences. I certainly am not with him there.

I had not intended to have touched upon the subject of thought transference in connection with a work dealing with so-called other-world manifestations ; but the fact that a great number of people not only associate telepathy with the alleged marvels, but, in certain cases, find in it a direct, or indirect, explanation of them, determines me to deal with the question. So, in the following chapter, I have at some length set forth my views and experiences in connection therewith.

I would say here that what is termed sub-consciousness is apt to play a not unimportant part with respect to certain phases of the phenomena. The reflex action of the brain is a wondrous thing, and its workings, if properly understood and given due credit, would, in ordinary, every-day life, go a long way towards making explicable what is apparently inexplicable.

One depends too much upon conscious memory without taking into consideration that which exists in a latent form, but which, in the recollections of the present, is overlooked.

It is astonishing how positive we can be that we have never heard of such and such a person or thing until a chord of recollection is touched, and the mind goes back, and that, which seemingly had no previous existence in one's remembrance, comes to be remembered.

On the other hand, how easy it is for some folk to believe in occurrences which, in the first instance, have had no more reality than that contained in a highly inventive imagination! Constant reiteration of the fictitious occurrence and the personal part played in connection therewith serves to make them real and personal to themselves.

It was said of my friend with whom I stayed at Clopton that, having purchased with the manor the portraits of members of the ancient family who were his predecessors in possession of the property, his constant association with these portraits and his description of them to his many visitors had finally caused him to look upon them as those of his own family, and that the Cavalier ghost who was reported to walk was, by sequence, an ancestor of his. Now, my friend was a bluff, kind-hearted man of the world, without an atom of side, and if such a conclusion existed at the back of his head, as it were, as hinted at, then it arose from verbal usage rather than from unwarranted assumption—which in fact, with him, would have been altogether unthinkable.

It was different with another friend whom I first met in Calcutta. He was just off tiger-shooting in the Himalayas. The season for tiger-shooting was over, but he assured me he was promised some good sport, and was determined to have it. He departed, and was away some weeks. On his return he related his adventures. They were of a somewhat startling character, and, in the end, he displayed for my admiration the skin of a tiger he had shot. It seemed to me not to have that freshness one would associate with an animal so recently slain, but, in my admiration of its real beauty, I let that pass. And then his story of his adventure was so realistic, and told with such evident conviction!

A few days later an enterprising merchant, from whom I had already made a few purchases, came and asked if I would like to buy a tiger-skin. I was not a buyer. With that insinuating, not-to-be-refused air peculiar to the East the dealer pressed me for all he was worth. It was a beautiful skin, the most beautiful in all India, of course. It was even finer than the one he had just sold my friend, the sportsman in the room opposite, and which I had seen. He said this with his finger to his lips, as if imparting a secret of the utmost importance. In the end the skin was unfolded for my inspection. It was indeed a splendid skin, finer even than the one my friend had undertaken such a hazardous expedition to obtain.

But I was not a buyer. I had neither the desire nor the ability to rival my friend in the matter of tiger-hunting stories, so, in finally refusing his tempting bargain, I delicately hinted that before again offering it in the same hotel he should wait until my friend had departed with his dearly-prized trophy. He took the hint, and my friend left Calcutta without the remotest suspicion that I was aware how he really obtained that skin, or the price he paid for it.

Some years afterwards I happened to be in a Midland town where my tiger-shooting friend, who had then received the honour of knighthood, resided. He was good enough to invite me to dinner. In the course of the evening my hostess said, " Oh, I had almost forgotten, but there is an old friend of yours which you must see before you go." And she took me to the study, where, perfectly mounted, with the finest glass-eyes imaginable, spread before the fireplace, was the identical tiger-skin I had seen in Calcutta. Several people were standing around, and one said to me, " Oh, you were with Sir William on that expedition, and know all about it."

I said nothing, but looked inquiringly at Sir William, who was leaning against the fireplace, legs astride, calmly puffing at a huge cigar.

" Quite so," he replied ; " but it's hardly fair to bring him in, as he, you know, had the first shot, and failed to kill. It is true it was a most difficult shot, but no one likes to be reminded of a failure of this kind."

"And you, happily, were more successful, dear," put in his wife, with admiration in her eyes; "a wounded tiger is, I should say, a dangerous beast."

"It was a near squeak, wasn't it?" said my host. He drew hard at his cigar as if seeking further inspiration.

"Never mind," he continued; "all's well that ends well, and here's the beast's skin as a lasting memento. He was a hard dier, anyway."

And so the story had put on fresh fringes, of which it appears I was one. And, without doubt, in the course of the telling Sir William had come to believe in the truth of it. He was a hard-headed man of business, of the strictest probity, and one whose word in ordinary matters could have been taken unhesitatingly. But this tiger story had become an obsession, and it is difficult to say what sort of mental shock or surgical operation would have put it in its true light.

This phase of mentality is not uncommon with a certain number of what are called "True Believers" in spiritism. They, like Sir William, who went out to bag his tiger and could not bring himself to return home empty-handed, in their desire for a sign, set out in life to bag something associated with the other world. But whereas Sir William did manage to annex a skin by way of showing what he had convinced himself he had accomplished, the sign-seekers, in making their claims to having succeeded in their spirit quest, fail to produce the slightest material proof of what they lay claim to. If one of those garment-attired spirits, so dear to the heart of a recent convert, would, on the occasion of her terrestrial visits, leave behind in the hands of the vision-seers the smallest article of celestial attire—even a spiritual bootlace—that would be something to go upon in the way of definite evidence. I trust the eminent novelist who advances the dress theory will see to this. As my tiger-hunting friend experienced no difficulty in getting his desire for a skin to exhibit to his friends satisfied, so, I fancy, would those vision-seers be able to obtain through professional mediumship any article they might wish as an outward and visible sign of the celestial visit they assert has been accorded them. A medium who has not hesitated to produce for the delectation of the faithful a fully materialised spirit form surely would not boggle at producing equally convincing spirit garments — at a price. They, no doubt, would be careful enough not to make a transfer of articles bearing a tell-tale earthly trade-mark.

Whilst there are those who at the beginning know full well that the supernatural phenomena of which they claim to have had actual experience have had no existence beyond expectation and the desire to be considered favoured above their fellows, and who in the course of constant reiteration come themselves to believe in the actuality of the alleged occurrences, there are others who are firmly convinced that they have experienced what they relate. They are quite honest in their beliefs, but also quite mistaken. They do not set themselves to examine, but seek all around them for confirmation, not explanation, of the phenomena which they, themselves not understanding, ascribe to supernatural causes. With time, following only this line of argument, conviction becomes more firmly established, and through this conviction others, equally unable to weigh and judge matters in this connection, become impressed. Folly is catching, and no form of folly is so infectious as this craze for the supernatural. And of all infectious diseases human nature is subject to, there is none more mentally disturbing, more physically debilitating, or more morally harmful than this one.

.   .   .   .   .   .

I thought it would come, and it has. Spirit airmen and spirit aeroplanes have been met with aloft ; so runs the latest story. It was to be expected in connection with the present supernatural wave. If the sea provides its sea-serpents, its Flying Dutchman, and other strange phenomena, why should not the skies provide their quota of the weird ? So it comes about that airmen in their flights have encountered winged air-dragons and mysterious shapes presumably possessing a supernatural affinity with the much-canvassed monsters of the deep. The Flying Dutchman of the sea has its counterpart in the mysterious, unclassed phantom-ship of the air.

What can't imagination cause some folk prone to self-deception to see, wherever they may be ? And with them, of course, there is no argument. You simply have to accept their statements as related, without question, or, as they put it, doubt their word. One doesn't wish to question their veracity. Give them all the credit for believing the accuracy of what they state, but, at the same time, question the correctness of their conclusions. It is not enough for them to believe to bring conviction. Something more than the description of what at the most has been a purely subjective vision is surely necessary.

Before modern spiritism came in with spooks at call at séances where so-called mediums presided, that other world of the supernaturally inclined provided mild excitement in the shape of ghosts that walked on such occasions and in such localities as seemed best to them. As a rule they attached themselves to the families of the aristocracy, but here and there a mere plebeian visitor from Ghostland, it is alleged, has put in an appearance, and in localities and under conditions which would have seemed to be uncongenial to ghostly visitations. This may be accounted for by the fact that those who have affected to see or hear them have themselves been somewhat low down in the social scale ; besides, in these democratic days, why should the blue-bloods have the monopoly of ghosts ? Anything so thoroughly reactionary is quite unthinkable !

Within a very few minutes' walk from the cottage on the Hampden estate where I write this is located, according to tradition, the scene of a ghostly visitation. It takes the form of a funeral *cortège* slowly wending its way up the historic glade to the church wherein John Hampden lies buried. Some say it is the ghost-burial of the great patriot, who after receiving his fatal wound on Chalgrove field was taken to Thame to die, his body afterwards being brought home to be buried.

I have not myself seen this ghostly procession, neither have I come across anyone who will claim to have done so ; but there are several old inhabitants who state that there must be some truth in the story which has been carried down to them first, second, or third hand, and, with much wise wagging of the head, they ask what one makes out of it. One story runs to the effect that a company of soldiers on the march encountered it, and, impressed with its reality, stood aside to let it pass. It, of course, is claimed that the soldiers previously knew nothing of the alleged ghostly visitation, and halted and stood aside in the full belief that it was a *bona fide* native funeral procession. Tradition, in handing down the story, omits to furnish any evidence on this point.

An adjacent estate—that of Lord Dormer—furnishes another ghost story. The visitation, it is alleged, takes the form of a ghostly lady, who, when she does happen to manifest, gives the vision-seer an exceedingly disagreeable shock. She gibbers and flits menacingly across the road, disappearing in the direction of the house. On such appearances she has had a bad effect upon horses and dogs as well as human beings. I have not been favoured with a sight of her, neither has my faithful companion and fellow-spook-seeker, my dog Peter. But I have met one man who claims to have seen the ghost, and, with great emphasis, he explained the shock both he and the mare he was driving had received when the visitation took place. I am inclined to the conclusion that he firmly believed what he said. Indeed he displayed great anxiety to hurry away from the hotel in Wycombe, where the narrative was made, before it got too late. "The ghost," he said, " came in with the moon as a rule, and the horse he was driving was very nervous and shy." A friend of mine who, whilst he had not himself seen the apparition, was well aware of the local belief therein, told him plainly not to be an ass, and suggested that the double whisky he was then lowering before closing time would be the only spirit he would see from then until he reached home. We offered to accompany him, but he refused. Later we drove over much the same ground as he had taken, but the apparition did not elect to put in an appearance. This was disappointing, especially, I fancy, to " Peter," who had no touch with the invisible beyond that afforded by a rustling rabbit in the undergrowth and the distant bark of a predatory fox—both very old and material indications of earthly visitations !

I never saw the ghost-seer again, and, for some time past, I have heard nothing about the ghostly lady's further appearances in the neighbourhood.

But ghosts, or spooks, or whatever you may choose to call them, have a habit of haunting this or that place as best may suit them, relying upon frail, gullible human nature to see justice done them in the matter of giving currency to their visitations.

They have odd ways, too, of manifesting themselves or of giving indications of their supernatural presence. The very latest, I should imagine, would be the outbreak near Folkestone, of which mention has been made in the press. These mysterious occurrences, one is given to understand, are engaging the serious attention of a distinguished novelist and an impressionable scientist who have identified themselves as believers in spiritualism and occult phenomena.

But the occurrences in question display no particularly new features. Things fly about, and sometimes people get hit. This has all happened before, and, spasmodically, has gone on merrily until the humans who worked the wonders have owned up or been tripped up, when the " phenomena " have ceased. If the eminent persons referred to in the newspapers were to employ their great talents in discovering the human agency causing the alleged phenomena, they would, I take it, arrive at an explanation more quickly than in seeking for a supernatural solution of them. But the highly imaginative gentleman who, in connection with these occurrences, sees a common or garden pickaxe go for him, after the pugnacious fashion of a Bolivian fighting snake, gets one completely !

It is a supernatural item full of dramatic possibilities, and as a turn at the Halls would draw all London. But since, one may expect to be told, a London atmosphere, or indeed any atmosphere outside of that where the phenomenon has its origin, would not suit, then I would willingly arrange for an audience to be brought to the spot, the proceeds to go to some deserving War charity. All I should require before making arrangements for a public demonstration would be a private rehearsal providing the necessary proof that the phenomenon had an existence beyond that furnished through the illusory imagination of the narrator.

Meanwhile, what may we not next expect in the matter of subjective phenomena which to the seer of them, and those too who lay themselves out to think with them, are so thoroughly convincing ?

.   .   .   .   .   .

So much for mental eccentricities, with the proneness of the dabblers in the occult to exaggeration and erroneous analysis. Now to the physical side of the emotions, as dealing with what one may term false sensorial impressions, where one is at once on firmer and more productive ground.

Repeatedly have I heard it stated by " sitters " at séances I have attended that not for a moment have they released the hands of the medium they have assuredly been holding during the occurrence of manifestations for which a spiritual origin has been claimed. In making this statement, such sitters have done so in the full

belief that the sitting was held under the conditions related. But they are mistaken. The
medium had got his hand free without their
knowing it. The sitter felt the medium's hand
upon his, but it was not the same hand with
which he was in touch at the beginning of the
séance. In the dark it is the easiest thing in
the world, by a series of nervous twitchings and
convulsive movements, to draw the hands nearer
together and to substitute, say, the left hand
for the right or the right for the left, as the
case may be, without the change—unseen by
the eye—being observed. In this way con-
tinual contact may readily be declared to have
existed during the whole of the séance. With
one hand thus freed, however, the medium is
enabled to work his wonders at will. I have
known them get both hands free, and thus
double the wonders of "spirit force." With
a hand thus free and a conveniently-got-at pair
of lazy tongs, objects can be manipulated at a
distance beyond the medium's ordinary reach,
and persons in the circle given that thrilling
touch so eagerly accepted by the faithful as a
special sign of spirit selection. A bit of sponge
dipped in phosphorus oil at the end of an adjust-
able telescopic-rod will provide the floating
spirit lights, and the finger of the medium fresh
from insertion in a bottle of ether afford that
cold, conclusive spirit touch so much sought after,
and appreciated, when on tap at dark séances.
Of course, the chief thing is for the medium to
temporarily free himself without the knowledge

of those sitting on either side of him being aware
of it. With this freedom much is possible in
the matter of wonder-working. Without it, or
failing the assistance of a helpful confederate,
there could be no manifestations. The spirits in
this direction can only do what the medium
himself can do, and when opportunities are
afforded him of so doing it.

Dark séances were invented by the mediums
for the purpose of affording them the desired
facilities for providing the manifestations sought
after. And again, sitters had a weakness for
séances held under these conditions. To have a
spirit thrill in the dark was far more fetching
than to receive one in broad daylight or under
the glare of the gas. Of course, when it came
to " form materialisations " a gentle, subdued
light was far more appropriate than total darkness, under which latter conditions it would not
be possible to recognise " appearances " with
certainty.

Spirits, so far as I can gather, have ever shown
a rooted dislike to materialising at séances in
full light. Materialising mediums, it goes without saying, lay down the conditions in accordance with their own convenience and ability to
work the oracle without detection, under which
visitors from the other world are able, and willing,
to appear. The spirits themselves, as manifesting
at these séances, sad to say, have no voice whatever in the matter.

It is astonishing how the senses can be falsified
when the eye cannot see what produces the effect.

11

In the dark, all sorts of false sensorial impressions are possible ; and, with blindfolded eyes, similar impressions can be obtained in the light by anyone conversant with the methods of the mediums and their ability to duplicate results obtained by them for which a spiritual origin has been claimed.

Again and again have I publicly demonstrated the possibility of this ; and whilst vast audiences have seen me get a hand free and work the miracles after the fashion adopted by the spirit-controlled medium, the blindfolded sitters, not seeing how and when it was done, have stoutly averred that not for a single moment has my hand left theirs.

Some years ago a very learned German scientist, Professor Zöllner of Leipzig, made—according to his own claims—a new scientific discovery, viz. a Fourth Dimension of Space. This permitted of the passage of one solid matter through another solid without damage or destruction to either. It was due to this that an iron ring placed upon the medium's head could be taken therefrom by spirit power and placed upon the Professor's own arm whilst firmly holding the two hands of the medium. By no other process than that of matter passing *through matter* could such a phenomenon be explained. I had the marvel demonstrated with myself—in the dark, of course. And I was at once convinced that not only did no spirit-hand remove the ring from my head, but that it was that of the medium, although to all sense of touch his hands when

once upon mine seemingly never left them, and
when my hands were firmly grasping his I felt
the ring on my arm. When the light went up
I examined the ring and found it solid enough.
But how did it get on my arm?

It certainly did not pass through it, neither
had the ring temporarily dematerialised to permit
of my arm passing through it.

A Fourth Dimension of Space? Another
unjustified conclusion by an otherwise learned
and presumably sane scientist! Just another
mediumistic fake, nothing else! It was the old,
old game of a false sensorial impression. The
medium so managed it as to impress upon the
sitter that both his hands were on his, whereas,
at any moment he desired it, he could, whilst
the impression lasted, free one hand, get possession of the ring, slip it on to his own arm, and,
when the sitter grasped the hand with all the
force he knew how, the ring slid on to the arm
of the sitter.

And this is precisely how matter passed through
matter.

After my experience of the " phenomenon "
I at once set myself to duplicate it under exactly
the same conditions, and have managed it with
unvarying success on, I should say, quite a thousand occasions. I can do it with a blindfolded
person in the light fully as well as in the dark,
only of course the expectancy, under such conditions, that spirit power has a part in it is absent.
But the false sensorial impression desired is created
all the same, and the ring gets on to the arm

without the least assistance of supernatural force. It is quite an interesting experiment, either in private or in public; and the solemn assurance of the one with whom it is made, that not for a second does a hand leave his, generally affords considerable amusement.

People should really not be so positive as to what they feel when they are not aided by their sight, neither should they be so confident as to the direction of sound. We are so apt to look about when a sudden or unexpected noise occurs, trying to find out with the eye what has produced it, that we depend more upon our sense of sight than that of hearing in determining the location of sound.

It is much the same with animals as with humans. My Scotch terrier "Peter," who is himself a bit of a thought-reader, the most sagacious animal I have ever known, is sixteen years old, and was with my R.E. son at Cambridge. His hearing is still exceedingly good, but his sight, I am grieved to say, is failing. Now, when he is called, he tries to gauge the direction of the call by sight; but failing to see any great distance, a bewildered, helpless look comes into his highly intelligent face, and he wanders aimlessly about, until by some process of deduction he acquires a sort of knowledge of his position. But his sense of smell remains practically unimpaired, and by scent he will follow unfalteringly in the country in my footsteps for miles. This same sense of smell or a dog's power of deduction is not given to humans, who, when they hear spirit voices and fail to locate the invisible forms, have nothing beyond the sense of sight to fall back upon to determine the location of the ghostly guides who, obviously, are not visible to the eye.

In a little experiment I publicly introduced many years ago for the purpose of testing the accuracy of the most acute of hearing in locating sound when the eye could not see the exact location of the sound produced, I have not yet found anyone, outside the blind, who has given anything approaching a correct indication of the locality. The blind seek to locate sound by sense of hearing and not by sight.

In the early days of my investigation of the occult there was, in Paris, a very prominent savant, Dr Charcot, who, scientifically and otherwise, had brought the art of suggestion in connection with the treatment of patients at his hospital to a more effective point than hitherto had been accomplished. But he permitted his enthusiasm to warp his judgment, and, despite his scientific attainments, not infrequently arrived at exceedingly erroneous conclusions.

His greatest successes were with female patients, and amongst them were some whom he claimed to be affected and influenced to an extraordinary extent by their contact with different metals. For instance, a band of gold placed over the arm would beget a condition of exaltation, one of silver severe depression, and one of copper intense horror. I saw the tests, and noted the various facial expressions and physical emotions produced by the metals' application. There was no questioning the results, but, to me, they did not appear to be the outcome of what was claimed for them. Given a similar expectancy, a similar belief, and the application of any other metals, in my opinion, would produce kindred effects. I laid emphasis upon this point of expectancy, and upon the knowledge of the patient of the nature of the metal with which she was brought in contact. This was met with the assertion that the most severe tests had been employed, and that it was the touch and feel of the metal itself which alone produced the emphatic mental and physical emotions indicated.

Just as some were abnormally affected and influenced by colour, so were others similarly influenced by metallic touch. With this assertion I was inclined to agree ; but, at the same time, I ventured to point out that the sense of sight played as important a part in the matter as the sense of touch. The patient had become obsessed with the belief that certain metals produced certain effects upon her. Her eye saw what metal was to be applied, and her expectancy, operating through a neurotic temperament, did the rest. When the patient could not see what ring of metal was placed over her arm, no result similar to that obtained when there was sight to assist was definitely demonstrated. There were mental and physical emotions, it is true, but they were frequently out of place, and showed that the patient was indulging in guesswork, and judging as much as possible by the weight of the encircling ring. It proved beyond doubt that the emotions were ever ready for the customary display, but that to be displayed in proper order they depended upon their cue, and the cue was the sense of seeing what the metal really was before the appropriate emotion could be awakened.

To logically demonstrate this I had rings, similar in shape and of the same weight as the metal circles actually used, moulded in plaster of Paris, painting them with solvents to represent the genuine metals. The patients being unaware of the manipulation, and seeing what was placed upon their wrists, proceeded to give off the anticipated emotions appropriate to the original tests.

Some of these patients were natural actresses, and the display of the emotions was not only well done, but naturally done. And, to this day, I am of opinion that they really believed they were subject to varied metallic influences, and that the emotions they displayed were the consequences of this influence.

That some people are materially influenced by colour—different colours producing different results—is unquestionable. In no place, according to my observation, was this feeling more pronounced than in Petrograd. But in the old days, in what was then the higher society, the belief was apt to assume an occult form, which, of course, was absurd.

Associated with this aspect of the matter I have in mind a most interesting meeting with a little circle of highly intellectual Grand Dukes and Grand Duchesses at Baden-Baden. One Imperial Highness, at whose palace I was to be entertained on my arrival in Petrograd, and who had maintained considerable interest in my work, was anxious to know how colour affected me ; but his curiosity in this direction was apparently far greater as to how it affected my relative, Miss Phyllis Bentley, who happened to be present on that occasion. His Imperial Highness was under the impression that she possessed some mysterious magnetic gift, although it had been placed beyond question that she had no such gift, and made no sort of claim to it. On the contrary, her duplications of the alleged magnetic phenomena of " Georgia Magnet " were simply a scientific application of the Diversion of Force.

But when that superstrong man amongst monarchs, the Tzar Alexander III., had, at that historic gathering of royalties at Castle Bernstorff, Copenhagen, failed to lift Miss Bentley from the ground, although exerting his full strength, the Russians, knowing their ruler's physical powers, were inclined to believe there was something magical or magnetic about it. The Tzar himself had no such illusions. He knew his strength had been diverted, but that it was through a scientific knowledge of how force could be diverted, and was not due to some special magnetic power.

But, apparently, what his Majesty clearly understood, others very closely associated with him did not understand.

So this particular Grand Duke went through

with Miss Bentley the various colours and the effect he had already determined, according to his assumption of her possession of magnetic powers, they would have upon her.

This was interesting enough in its way ; but his Imperial Highness had arrived at a further, and quite impossible, conclusion in the shape of her being equally influenced at a distance by a colour which she could not see, but the peculiar personal attributes of which would be magnetically conveyed and felt.

He suggested that, the next morning, he should call her up at the telephone, and she could tell him what colour he held, and the effect produced thereby. " I will not," he concluded, " hold up a yellow, as that colour, I am convinced, would most adversely affect you."

The dear old gentleman! one could but humour him, and the test was conducted as he desired. But, it goes without saying, it was not a success.

Miss Bentley at the other end of the telephone had not the remotest idea what colour his Imperial Highness was handling, and was not, in the remotest degree, influenced thereby.

CHAPTER IX

THE POSSIBILITIES AND IMPOSSIBILITIES OF THOUGHT TRANSFERENCE

WHEN I set out to write this book on "other-world" phenomena and the various false premises and wilful impostures that went with them, I had no intention of touching upon the mind-reading aspect of the question. To this subject of mind-reading, with which I have been closely associated for very many years, I have already devoted much space in other works I have inflicted upon the public. The tendency, however, in certain quarters to provide an explanation for certain phases of the supernatural, arising out of "other-world" manifestations, causes me to go into the matter at a length which I hope will be found excusable.

I would at once say that I have no more belief in the marvels of so-called thought transference than I have in supernatural phenomena. Thought transference has its limits, and, beyond a certain point, there is nothing doing.

There are inquirers into the supernatural who, whilst disinclined to accept spirit influence as an explanation of certain phenomena, are disposed to find a solution in telepathic communication between medium and subject. Such telepathic communication does not, and cannot, take place, and it therefore in no way provides a solution of that which the inquirer erroneously assumes is open to no other explication. The acceptor of the thought-transference theory builds up a wonderful idea of waves of thought carrying with them, subconsciously, illuminative details from the investigator to the seer, assumedly whilst in touch with the other world.

It is just as possible for such a passage of thought as it is for the earthly visitation of a disembodied spirit. One is as impalpable and ungraspable a commodity as the other.

It is not the subconscious thought relying upon a message-carrying brain-wave that conveys the desired information to the medium.

The medium is not on the look-out for such non-existent brain passages. He is incapable of receiving them, or interpreting them had they any existence. He is quite content with the old, old game of putting fishing questions, of hazarding statements and watching the effect produced. Mediums, as a rule, are remarkably wide-awake individuals—even when in a trance condition— and exceedingly good judges of character. Experience enables them to immediately weigh and appraise facial and other physical indications unconsciously manifested by their sign-seeking clients. The clients give them physically clues which non-existent brain-waves are incapable of conveying.

Why will people mistake keenness of perception and the ability to read character for the possession of some abnormal mental gift enabling the possessor thereof to get at the hidden inner thoughts of his fellows as readily as the out-and-out medium can establish communication with celestial denizens of the Unseen World ? The mind of man can be read, but not on the basis of what is termed telepathy. Study the subject, pursue it night and day, anywhere, everywhere, and you will never get beyond a certain point. The mind is encased in matter, and readable only by and through that matter. You can no more hold and analyse a brain-wave than you can a sunbeam, which, for its part, however, is more substantial to the extent of having for the time being a visible existence. Believers in thought transference will tell you how they visualise things, and that this visualisation is seeable and readable between two minds beating as one. Sheer phantasy ! It is all very well for a visualiser to, as he terms it, visualise things, but such visualisation conveys no decipherable picture to another. At the commencement of the mind-reading furore an exceedingly astute Yankee, who spoiled his chances of success by unjustifiable claims to powers which he certainly did not possess, claimed to read in the retina of his "subject's" eye the mental picture such "subject" had centred his thoughts upon. This, and pretences of a similar character, got the back up of the scientific world, and he was severely criticised accordingly. Dr Brudenell Carter, the eminent

oculist, was an exceptionally bitter critic. As
he explained to me, the retina was as incapable
of containing, or conveying, a mental picture
as, for instance, a lump of coal.

Mr Henry Labouchere, too, was moved to
wrath over the American seer's pretensions, and
trounced him severely in *Truth*. A libel action
was the outcome of these attacks, but the plaintiff
thought fit to withdraw therefrom before it came
on for hearing. I was subpœnaed as a witness by
my very good friend Sir George Lewis, acting on
behalf of Mr Labouchere. In connection with
the serving of this subpœna an amusing incident
occurred. The emissary of Messrs Lewis thought
fit to serve me at the Princes' Hall, Piccadilly,
where I was giving a public representation. My
chairman that evening was the Marquis of Lorne.
There was generally assumed to exist a strong personal resemblance between the Marquis and myself ; indeed, in Court circles I was known as " the
Double." So, during the interval, the representative of Messrs Lewis & Lewis, mistaking the
Marquis for myself, politely desired to present him
with the subpœna and a guinea caution-money.

" No, no," said the Marquis laughingly,
" honour and the guinea to whom they are due !
This "(indicating me) "is your man. Now, had
you been a thought-reader like my friend here,
the superiority and difference would have been
quite clear to you."

One of the last letters I had from the late
Duke of Argyll, oddly enough, had reference to
this likeness. He wrote :

" MY DEAR BUT SUPERIOR DOUBLE,—A very queer
thing happened last night. A man whom I didn't know
from Adam persisted in nodding to me and seeking to
draw me aside into conversation. At last I said : ' My
dear sir, I am afraid you have made a slight mistake,
for really I haven't the pleasure of knowing you.' To
this he replied with some warmth : ' Not know me !
why, d—— it all, man, you, Stuart Cumberland, to say
you don't know *me* ! ' "

A further mix-up of personalities oddly enough
occurred at another meeting of mine at Princes'
Hall. My chairman on that occasion was Mr
J. W. Lowther (later to become the Speaker),
and I announced that fact.

With this announcement a horsey-looking man
got up from his seat and, with an indignant snort,
exclaimed : " Tell us another. That Jimmy
Lowther ? not much ! I know him too well to
be taken in like this."

" I am indeed James Lowther," said my chairman with a smile, " and sometimes, I fancy, I am
called Jimmy, but I am not the Jimmy you have
in your mind. I happen to know him too, and
I can well understand your disappointment in not
finding the man so much after your own heart
occupying the post of prominence this afternoon."

There was an all-round laugh, and the man sat
down, but in his heart I felt sure he would much
rather have seen the Jimmy Lowther of sporting
fame occupying Mr Speaker's chair on the platform than any experiments I had to present to
the audience.

To return to the Yankee mind-reader. When

Mr Labouchere had taken so decided a line antagonistic to thought-reading, I felt that the only way to convince him of what was really possible and genuine in the art was to take him as a " subject." With this object in view I called on him at his residence in Queen Anne's Gate.

" And so you wish to read my thoughts ? " he remarked, as he leant against the fireplace smoking a cigarette.

I told him that I not only wished to do so, but that, with his permission, I was going to have a good try to succeed.

" Go ahead. What am I thinking of now ? "

" Well, in the first place, I should say you are thinking that I cannot succeed."

" Not a bad shot," was the cynical rejoinder, " and one which required no thought-reading powers and preconceived ideas to arrive at."

" Quite so ; but," I added, " if you will concentrate your entire thoughts for a moment upon some concrete object in this room, I will endeavour to indicate what you have fixed your mind upon."

" It is done," replied Labby.

I therefore took him, and succeeded in finding the object thought of. Mr Labouchere did not prove an ideal " subject " ; indeed a more placid, emotionless one I had never previously experimented with. But he was quite honest about the test, and frankly admitted that thought-reading, as I illustrated it, was genuine enough.

As I was removing my blindfold there was a knock at the door, and a grimy apparition stood

hesitatingly in the doorway carrying a coal-
scuttle.

"I beg your pardon, sir, but I've come to make
up the fire," said the slavey, regarding me with
unfeigned curiosity.

"All right, go ahead. Now," added Labby
to me in an aside, "here's your chance. See
what you can make of her. She has never heard
about nor read about thought-reading, and has, I
dare say, about as much mental concentration as
a cockroach. It will be interesting to see what
you make of her."

Then turning to the maid, who had deposited
her coal-scuttle by the fireplace, he remarked :
"You see this gentleman. Well, he has been
finding things I had hid in this room, and telling
me things I thought no one but myself knew.
Have you any idea who he is ? "

" No, sir."

" Can't you guess ? "

" He ain't a burglar or a detective, is he ? "

" No, no, my girl ; worse, far worse than either,
although he doesn't look it. He is what they
call a magician. You've heard of magicians, I
suppose ? "

" Them as can turn a person into a black cat,
and swaller 'ot coals as if they was lollipops. I've
'eard on 'em, sir."

" No, this gentleman is a new sort of wizard,
my girl," replied Labby. " He sort of turns you
inside out before you know where you are, and
tells you just what you are thinking about and
all that sort of thing."

"I am sure I've nothink to 'ide," broke in the girl. "I 'ad the best of characters from my last place, and whilst I've bin 'ere I think, sir, I've given every satisfaction."

"Quite so," said Labby soothingly. "But will you think of something that you would like my friend to try and find for you?"

"That I will, sir. I find I've just lost somethink, and perhaps 'e could find it for me."

"But she must know where it is," I put in, "as I can't find what she doesn't know."

"I can give a pretty good guess, sir, where it dropped."

I took the girl, and found a little brooch which had fallen in the coal-scuttle she had been carrying.

"Thank you, that will do," said Labby, as the poor little trembling subject stood agape, fearing she might after all be turned into a black cat, and the maid beat a retreat, to relate downstairs the "wonder" she had experienced in the room she had just left.

In the course of other experiments subsequently performed with Mr Labouchere the editor of *Truth* became not only fully convinced of the possibilities of getting at thought on the basis of my experiments, but he became one of my most enthusiastic supporters in my crusades against shams and impostures, and endeavours to advance scientific truth.

It was he who arranged for me that historic séance in the House of Commons, at which the then Premier, Mr W. E. Gladstone, was the principal " subject."

The séance was held in the smoking-room, and representatives of all parties were present. As the Premier crossed over to me on entering the room, Mr Tim Healy, who was sitting with out-stretched legs in a chair close by, arose with alacrity and, with marked politeness, offered Mr Gladstone his seat. This, however, the Premier politely declined. Considering the tension then existing between the Government and the Irish party, the act of Mr Healy, which arose solely from natural courtesy, was, I remember, much canvassed at the moment. Indeed, an illustrated paper in illustrating the séance had a sketch of the brilliant Irishman offering his seat to his political oppressor, with the headline, " Extremes meet."

The most interesting experiment I performed with Mr Gladstone was in putting down on a sheet of paper pinned to the wall some figures upon which the G.O.M. had centred his thoughts. I began with a 3, which my subject said was correct. This was followed by 6 ; also correct. The next figure thought of was 5 ; but no sooner was it on the paper than I noticed that Mr Gladstone had changed his mind, and that he had replaced in his mind the 5 by a 6. I therefore struck out the 5 and put down the 6, declaring the figures thought of to be 366.

This my subject admitted to be perfectly correct. I asked him why he had changed his original thought of 365 to 366, and he said that at first he had thought of 365, the number of days in the year ; but, when I had got the 3 and 6, it dawned upon him that I might by sequence guess the remaining figure ; but, remembering it was leap-year, and that there were 366 days in the year, instead of 365, he had substituted the final 6 for the 5. "And," he concluded, with some enthusiasm, "you successfully read both phases of thought."

Mr Gladstone was a singularly emotional man, and physically felt and expressed every dominating idea. He had a remarkably magnetic personality, and the influence he at times exercised over others was almost mesmeric. It was his habit to visualise things, as it were ; but he frequently made the mistake of thinking that what under such conditions was perfectly clear and visible to him, should be equally clear and visible to others. And it often was not so. It was his habit, too, to dive deeply into things, and his general inside knowledge was indeed extraordinary. He was a sort of mental mercurial plate, absorbing all golden grains of information and knowledge with which he came in contact. Mentally, however, he was inclined to be somewhat in the cloud, with one end of his rainbow-like intellect touching *terra firma*, and the other losing itself in nebulous inconclusiveness.

Mr Gladstone was proud of being called the People's William ; but as Mr Labouchere, who after the séance discussed my reading of the Premier, remarked, "He lacks that touch of practical human nature that makes for complete understanding and popularity. If, for instance, like old Pam, he would only put a straw in his mouth and go to the Derby, he indeed would be the People's Idol, with no one to rival him."

It has been hinted that Mr Gladstone was a believer in spiritism. With me he never discussed the subject, and, from personal knowledge, I am unable to say what truth, if any at all, there was in the suggestion.

Mr Gladstone was a deeply religious man, of highly strung temperament, with a leaning towards the idealistic rather than the practical, and not unlikely to be carried away by his momentary emotions.

He, I do know, was somewhat superstitious, and not a little nervous.

He was good enough to take an interest in my writings, and I sent him an advance copy of a weird little story called *A Fatal Affinity*, which, in connection with the mystic vein that ran through it, I fancied might have some interest for him.

I received a post-card thanking me for the book, but nothing more. Some time afterwards I happened to meet Mrs Gladstone, who met me with a charming smile but a reproving shake of the finger. "Oh, you dreadful man!" she said banteringly. "That perfectly awful book you sent my husband has made him look under the bed every night before retiring ; and he hasn't done such a thing for years."

I don't suppose Mr Gladstone for a moment anticipated seeing the crouching astral form, figuring in the romance, underneath the bed ; but in the early days of his boyhood he may have acquired that habit in association with spectral fancies, and it had stuck to him through the years, to be reawakened by the trend of the story I had sent to him.

I am, by the by, inclined to regard the late Mr Labouchere in the rôle of a cynic as somewhat of a *poseur*. He was at heart a most kindly, helpful man, and countless untold good deeds stand to his credit.

He hated shams and pretences in all branches of life, and was a fearless and relentless critic of those who carried on any form of imposture. His exposures were good for the public, however crushing they may have proved to those who traded upon public credulity. Were he alive to-day, he would be with me in laying bare the pernicious claims to the supernatural which, unfortunately, have found such ready acceptance in certain quarters so sadly lacking in proper discrimination.

As he used to say, with withering sarcasm, of the second-sight and clairvoyant fraternity : " They can describe with marvellous clearness what has never happened at the other end of the world, and see through a brick wall as clearly as through a sieve, and yet not one of them can lay his hands upon the thousand pounds I am prepared to pay for the reading of a name written on a slip of paper placed in a sealed box."

Labby knew the full powers of these pretenders to occult gifts when he made this wager.

I may mention in connection with this meeting of the "extremes" that Mr T. P. O'Connor, who was present at the séance, had sent an account of it to the Irish papers with which he was associated, gracefully referring to the innate courtesy of the Irishman which permits him to put politeness before political antagonism. This little flash of geniality was, I believe, misunderstood, some going to the length of assuming that what Tay Pay meant to convey—and nothing was further from his thoughts—was that Tim Healy's display of natural politeness was an outward and visible sign of bowing the knee to the Sassenach Premier.

The years went by, until one night I was dining with Mr T. P. O'Connor at the House, and on our way to the smoking-room he was referring to my experiment with Mr Gladstone and to the meeting of the G.O.M. and Mr Healy, about which he had written. When we arrived in the smoking-room I said to my host, pointing to a particular part of the wall, " It was there I put up the paper upon which I wrote the figures thought of by Mr Gladstone."

" That's so ; I remember it well," replied Tay Pay.

And as I glanced around me, seated in the same place from which he rose to offer his seat to Mr Gladstone was Tim Healy.

Now, those occultly inclined will see in this a striking instance of thought transference, or the interposition of some out-of-the-way power not to be explained by ordinary means. And it was but a curious coincidence—that, and nothing more.

These professors of the occult invariably break down when put to the test. Occultism is built too much upon shadows to satisfy practical examination or conform to logical common-sense tests.

And yet people, as a rule, would much rather ascribe a mysterious, unknown force to things which happen, or which they assume have happened, than seek for an explanation of them in the purely natural. This has always astonished and frequently amused or annoyed me. It has been astonishing to find so much credulity, amusing to come across so much flimsy cocksureness, and annoying to find argumentative stupidity contradicting the plain findings of convincing common-sense.

So very often have I found folk crediting me with powers that not only I did not possess, but that I never had the remotest idea of laying claim to.

From the beginning I was content with such success as I achieved through gifts common to many and by means open to anyone. To claim or imagine there was anything uncanny about the matter never once entered my head. I knew I had an exceptional delicacy of touch and a somewhat abnormal keenness of perception. Added to this, I have been blessed with a truly remarkable memory, which has enabled me to draw upon my recollections at opportune moments for the correct interpretation of indi-

cations and the fitting in of conclusions previously
derived under similar conditions and with similarly
mentally constituted "subjects." I had, too,
complete faith in my star, and the will to win
under every conceivable condition. This em-
boldened me to take, as it were, my tent and set
it up in the high places and low places of the
great world, drawing my subjects and my audiences
alike from the high-born and the lowly. I have
been to countries where I have not spoken a
word of their language and have had to make
myself understood to miscellaneous audiences,
frequently of vast dimensions, through the
medium of an interpreter—often a faulty and
never a wholly satisfactory form of elucidation.
I have written down words in characters that at
the time have been wholly unintelligible to me,
just because the subject thought it was how they
should be written. I have experimented with
men of all ranks, nationalities, and colours; and
whilst in the main I have found human nature
very akin, different races have not only different
ways of thinking, but also diverse ways of giving
physical expression to their thoughts. For my
purposes I have found the Chinese and the Red
Indians the most emotionless of "subjects," and,
consequently, the most difficult to obtain accurate
physical indications from.

With all my experiences with so many peoples
in so many lands, it should go without saying
that had there been any direct way of getting at
thoughts other than by obtaining indications of
them through physical contact or making deduc-

tions from physical expressions I should most certainly have seized it, if only to have saved myself trouble and exertion. But my experience has taught me there is no such royal road to the mind as the believers in telepathy would appear to imagine ; and the silly talk about thought transference, and the assumption of occult powers, by way of accounting for what at best is happy guesswork or the outcome of some phase of curious coincidence, irritates me exceedingly. Nothing breaks down one's patience so much as stupidity's false conclusions.

The proneness of human nature to claim some mysterious, abnormal gift, and to see such gifts in others, is indeed remarkable. There is, apparently, something unsatisfying in the purely natural, and the stronger fare of supernatural pretence is required to tickle the appetite and satisfy the emotions. With such miracle-ruling folk I, obviously, in no way fill the bill. In what I do, I neither assume nor pretend enough. To say one reads thought only through physical expression, is to put what they would term mental wonders upon too commonplace a plane. The twaddle about thought transference and telepathic tall-talk are more congenial and convincing.

In their desire to invest everything with magical attributes, people will see in quite a commonplace occurrence proof of abnormal powers. Of this the following provides a very striking instance :—

Sir W. S. Gilbert, who was my chairman as well as one of my " subjects " at a representation

I gave at the Prince of Wales's Theatre, thought out a little drama in which he cast himself as the villain of the piece.   In fancy he was to commit forgery and to fly with the proceeds to some distant and more or less inaccessible spot.

The amount Sir William went for was £1,000,000, and the place he elected to take his plunder to was the Seychelles. I readily got at the amount, and, without difficulty, located the place on an enlarged map of the world fixed at the back of the stage.   " Quite correct," said Sir William when I had finished.   Then, with one of those sudden flashes of wit with which his conversation was frequently illuminated, he added, " Had I known my geography as well as Mr Cumberland I should have chosen a more home-from-home spot to which to retire, as I now notice the Gilbert Group is conveniently close, and for a moment Mr Cumberland, I observed, hesitated over stopping there."

What happened was this : in passing my hand over the map I noticed the minute dots thereon described as the Gilbert Group, and immediately I thought what an appropriate spot for a Gilbert to choose as a hiding-place ; but Sir William until that moment had not given the group a thought, having solely concentrated his mind upon the Seychelle Isles.

But this simple explanation, I found, did not satisfy those who saw in it the tapping of an unconscious hidden thought through the reading of a mental picture formed by my subject.

It was useless to say that I saw no mental

picture, there being no mental picture to see, and, as a matter of fact, the Gilbert Group never once entered Sir William's mind until I momentarily paused at its position on the map.

Yet one more, and concluding, instance of the assumed mental picture theory advanced in association with my experiments. It arose out of a test with Mr Cecil Rhodes. The "Empire Builder" had thought of a place the name of which he desired me to write down. I wrote "Thebes," which was correct. But, after I had written down the name, I found my "subject" thinking of some hieroglyphics, and these I drew roughly beneath the name I had written. Mr Rhodes had recently visited Egypt, and in thinking of Thebes, his thoughts ran on the quaint hieroglyphics associated with Egypt's ancient grandeur. I got no mental picture of this passing thought. I simply felt that Mr Rhodes had in his mind something to convey beyond the mere name of the place selected, and the hand I held conveyed the impression and the form of the characters I set down on the paper.

I would repeat that I am not responsible for the powers with which the mystically-inclined folk think fit to invest me. The credulous must think as they like. However, at all my public meetings and in all my writings I have clearly stated the basis upon which I operated, and which, in my opinion, was the only one by which results with anything approaching scientific accuracy could be arrived at.

At an early period of my career I published an

article in the *Nineteenth Century* clearly defining my views on the matter; and although I have travelled much since then, and have added considerably to my illustrations of thought-reading, I have not advanced a single step further in getting at thought by any other means than those I had at that time adopted.

Whilst practice certainly enables one to form a more complete opinion of man's mental complexity, the ability to successfully perform the experiments does not weaken with disuse. I had not given any public illustrations for many years until last year, when my friend Mr Oswald Stoll kindly arranged an agreeably successful séance for me at the Savoy Hotel. I afterwards gave a public representation before a monster audience at the Palace Theatre, Leicester, in aid of the War Seal Fund, in which deserving charity Mr Stoll has deeply interested himself.

In my time I have been associated with certain somewhat delicate political and diplomatic matters, and I certainly have found my knowledge of character of real use in this direction. It is curious how even the most hardened prevaricator and astute manipulator of words used for the purpose of conveying deception will give himself away by some unconscious little physical indication that belies his utterances. The eyes, the mouth, the hands, even (as with bootless peoples) the toes, have a tale to tell, and are readable by those who know how to interpret such indications or make correct deductions from them.

It is these physical indications unconsciously given off by sign-seekers under the close scrutiny and pumping process adopted by mediums which enable the mystic fraternity to occasionally correctly tumble on to " other-world " information. People, as a rule, never seem to know how liable they are to give themselves away in this manner, and, consequently, how frequently they do so.

To assume that telepathic communication takes place between the sign-seeker and medium is to assume what is not only improbable, but impossible. Communicative brain-waves no more pass between medium and client than between professional artists engaged in a " thought transference " music-hall turn. When these artists do not claim psychic powers, and in such a way feed the cravings of the credulous for injurious mystic fallacies, they provide a show that is both entertaining and attractive ; but there is no more transference of thought about the exhibition than passes between the conductor and his band. He provides the cues which his band interprets, just as the entertainer in the audience conveys the cues either by verbal or physical code to the interpreter thereof seated on the stage.

It is a business that requires considerable intelligence, a great deal of practice, and unlimited patience plus a most retentive memory. It is a pity that believers in the occult should advance the results achieved in this direction as proof of thought transference, as it goes towards antagonising science against an attractive, and at the same time puzzling, entertainment that, free from mystic pretensions, is innocent enough in all conscience.

.   .   .   .   .   .

A few words as to the psychology of nations, about which political *quidnuncs* write so voluminously and understand so little.

We will agree that Germany does not understand the psychology of the Allies; and this doubtless, in a measure, accounts for the misreading of our purposes and aims, and the stupendous blunders they commit in consequence thereof. But what nation, alien in blood and language, really understands the psychology of another?

The two nations, of all the nations of the world, best able to understand the psychology of each other are the United States and ourselves. We think on the same mental plane, and give utterance to our thoughts in a language at once understandable to each other.

With other nations thought has only too often to go through a process of translation before a common understanding is arrived at; and, in the course of translation, adjustments of mental reservations and other fitting-in of ideas have to be fixed up, all making for delay. Between the Americans and the British all is plain mental sailing from the start, and no phase of translation enters into the conversations and negotiations that take place between them. It is one thing for a man to be able to speak your language, and quite another for him to think in it. What he invariably does is to think it out in his own language, then to mentally translate it into what he assumes to be the equivalent language he is about to put into words.

The psychology of nations has had a supreme fascination for me, and how hard I have tried to fathom and understand that of each with which I have come in contact! Whilst in many lands I have had to get along with such scant knowledge of their languages as I might possess, or get my views publicly presented there through the medium of an interpreter—never a wholly satisfactory proceeding outside of our own Over Sea Possessions—the United States is the only country where I have been able to speak my mother-tongue with the certainty of being fully understood.

And as it has been with peoples as a whole, so has it been with representatives of these peoples. For instance, whilst I have successfully read the thoughts of men of prominence of different nationalities, such as Moltke, Alexandre Dumas fils, the ex-Khedive, Rubinstein, and Sagasta, each one understanding English, not one thought in my language, but in the one that came the most natural or the handiest to him. Whereas, when I first visited the States and experimented, for instance, with Henry Ward Beecher, J. G. Whittier, Oliver Wendell Holmes, and Boyle O'Reilly, they not only spoke in my language, but thought in it too. There is that psychological affinity between Americans and British which has no like existence between any other two peoples on earth. It is an affinity of feeling as well as of understanding.

I have been in more than one tight corner in the course of my travels, and my first thought if I had needed help would have been to have asked if there were a Britisher present to stand by me, and, failing him, an American, with the certainty that no cry of mine would have fallen on American ears unheeded. The thought of calling upon any other national outside of these two never occurred to me.

On one occasion, in a foreign land, a quarrel was forced on me, and a challenge to a duel was the outcome of it. There was no Britisher at hand to stand by me ; but an American consul, who, from his official position, could not act for me, thoughtfully, and very kindly, provided seconds for me in the persons of his two sons, who, as he said with due *naïveté*, were visiting him " quite unofficially."

.   .   .   .   .   .

One of the most interesting psychological studies known to me in the New World is undoubtedly Sir Wilfrid Laurier.

To understand Sir Wilfrid's attitude over the Canadian Military Service Act, which has aroused such deep and mixed feelings, one must understand the psychology of the man. He is mentally and physically emotional, easily read from the surface, but an inside reading of whom is by no means so easy. I have known Sir Wilfrid many years, and he was one of my earliest " subjects " amongst Canadians. The psychology of the man interested me immensely, and I was greatly attracted by his magnetic personality. Then he was just mounting the ladder to prominence and popularity. His verbal fervour was indeed remarkable, added to which was a personal magnetism of exceptional force and charm.

But all these gifts for the most part were centred in the interests of French Canada, with but a passing thought for the claims and aims of the rest of the Dominion. While this brought him into direct political conflict with the great Imperialist Sir John A. Macdonald, it, at the same time, obtained for him vast popularity and a practically unequalled influence amongst his fellow French Canadians.

Sir Wilfrid of the "silver tongue" speaks equally freely and eloquently in English and French. I have heard him in both languages many times, but never once have I found him thinking in English. He thinks always in French—the French of Louis XV.; and his spoken English is the verbal outcome of a rapid mental translation.

Throughout his political life his creed has ever been "Canada—my country—first." But with him, be it understood, "my country" begins and ends with the purely French thinking and speaking sections of Canada as distinct from that greater portion which goes to make up the Dominion.

With this mental outlook it has scarcely been possible for Sir Wilfrid Laurier to "think Imperially." But it would be a mistake for a moment to question his loyalty to the Mother Country, or to assume that he harbours any antagonism to the Imperial idea. He is all for the Empire having

13

the first place in the sun ; but, at the same time, that section of it, comprising the Province of Quebec, should have the benefit of the fullest extent of warmth to be derived from the sun. This idea ever causes him to put French Canada in the limelight. The rest just fits in with the picture he mentally draws.

It governs him in everything. When I wrote my descriptive history of Canada, *The Queen's Highway from Ocean to Ocean*, Sir John A. Macdonald was pleased to say, " Your work deserves the lasting gratitude of the people of Canada"; but Sir Wilfrid, who was otherwise personally well disposed towards me, felt I had made too much of the west and too little of French Canada. In a word, I was too Imperialistically expansive.

This absence of the expansive idea in Sir Wilfrid's temperament and mental outlook must not cause him to be bracketed with M. Henri Bourassa, who is really antagonistic to it. This political firebrand is politically and psychologically a French-Canadian Valera ; and as long as he can rule the roost amongst his French-Canadian Sinn Feiners, the welfare of the Empire as a whole is, I fancy, a matter of complete indifference to him. He began waving the red flag of revolt over Canada's suggested contribution to naval defence, and to-day Sir Wilfrid, unless he has strangely changed of late, cannot hold with Bourassa in his indifference to Germany's aims of conquest and domination. I say this, having in memory what Sir Wilfrid Laurier said to me in London shortly after the Kaiser's dispatch to Kruger : " Little Willie," said he, " has a bad fit of swelled head, and has got to be put in his place ; and I guess we'll do it."

The recent action of Sir Wilfrid, at an exceedingly critical period of the war, with the whole civilised world longing for the putting of the Kaiser in his place, surely was not the way to expedite it.

But then, again, one must understand the psychology of the man.

.   .   .   .   .   .

I have already referred to Sir Wilfrid's personal magnetism.   A word as to his electrically charged physical system.   When I was staying at the Russell Hotel, Ottawa, it was a familiar after-dinner amusement to see what electric discharges one could produce by coming suddenly in physical contact with each other.   Frequently I have lit the gas through Sir Wilfrid acting as the conductor, with his finger over the jet.   The plan adopted was to run quickly across the room, whilst Sir Wilfrid stood on a chair, the finger of one hand over the gas jet, and to touch his other hand with one's finger at the end of one's run.   I have produced the same effect when a chain of hands has been between me and the distinguished French-Canadian politician.

There was nothing spiritistic about this ; and the effects produced had no connection with other-world manifestations, although doubtless illogical sign-seekers would have seen in the occurrence direct evidence of supernaturalism. Anyone, more or less, could bring about similar results. It was the outcome of intense cold without and a highly heated atmosphere within the hotel. To come suddenly in contact hand to hand with another person in the room was to create a spark with a pin-prick feeling going with it. It was the same if the lips met or noses touched.

I did not try the process of rubbing noses, a form of affection in vogue with certain tribes of primitive love-making instincts ; but I am free to confess that the reminder of the thorn-protected rose is mild indeed as compared with the pricking spark emanating from the electrically environed kiss.

CHAPTER X

Is there anything underlying this latest spiritualistic movement beyond that provided by the
emotional longings arising out of the Great War
and mediumistic desire to make money out of
the craze ?

Can it by any possibility be that the enemy
has been making use of the movement for its
own purposes ?

The Hidden Hand, it is generally assumed,
has been at work in this country as well as in
those other countries where drastic unmasking
has taken place. Germany, for political and
military ends, uses strange tools, and turns to
her advantage every possible opportunity.

With the opportunities which may from time
to time present themselves in association with a
craze of this character, the employment of the
Unseen Hand in the Unseen World does not
appear to be entirely out of the question.

One knows that the enemy made every use of
that mystic impostor Rasputin, and that information of the first importance was obtained through
this channel, whilst, in addition, this mystic tool,
through the influence he possessed owing to his

claims to supernatural powers, was able to convey impressions and bring about results desired by his Teutonic instigators.

At the time of writing, *l'affaire Bolo* and *l'affaire Caillaux*—Caillaux, the "Man of Destiny"—are much in evidence in association with enemy intrigues; but, obviously, one would not be justified in anticipating any decision relating thereto. That rests alone with the authorities.

Just as the Germans made use of the seer Rasputin and the vicious mystic circle surrounding him, it would, however, be permissible to inquire as to the subtle propaganda worked by the enemy through mystic circles in Paris and Rome.

Some of the personages prominently associated with the two *affaires* have mystic temperaments, and have had associations with alleged occult wonder-workers.

The ultra-patriotic Madame de Thèbes, the much-discussed Parisian *devinette*, wielded considerable influence in French political and financial circles, besides being a pet of high society. To her went statesmen and high military and financial authorities for prophetic information, and, doubtless, in the course of such consultations unconsciously vouchsafed more information to the seeress than she was in a position to give them.

Madame de Thèbes specialised in war prophecies; but, as she possessed no more power of correctly divining the future than the silver-seeking clairvoyante of a London suburb, her prophecies had a habit of going wrong. They were based upon what she wheedled out of her clients, or what they lightly and unguardedly let fall, and her natural astuteness did the rest. Oracular utterances, based upon nothing more than human deductions, are sadly fallible ; and Madame de Thèbes, whilst she succeeded in imposing upon the credulous, and at the same time, presumably, did remarkably well out of her mystic pretensions, was anything but infallible. Now that she has left this world for that other world of her imaginings, she may acquire a more correct and intimate knowledge of the mysteries upon which she so successfully traded.

If, as it has been assumed, the enemy was not slow to turn to account the opportunities afforded by adroit manipulation of mystic materials to hand in association with Madame de Thèbes' consultations, similar opportunities to be worked through mystic channels in this country would not be altogether neglected.

The Hidden Hand of the enemy is difficult to trace, and one would scarcely look for it in association with the spiritual world. But the spiritual world in this mundane sphere is made up of human follies, human weaknesses, vanities, and greed. Credulous folk seeking consolation, advice, or information through the medium of the supernatural are none too wise in their inquiries nor guarded in their utterances.

It will have been very easy for German agents or sympathisers to have obtained useful information under such circumstances. Service men and the relations of those connected with the Services have formed a very considerable proportion of the professional mystics' *clientèle*, and nearly all the inquiries and sign-seeking instincts of these people have had reference to matters associated directly or indirectly with the war.   Given such a *clientèle*, providing the necessary elements of credulity, silliness, and tactlessness, what then could be easier, on the part of an astute medium, than the exploitation of such material for all it was worth ?

I have seen the possibilities in such a situation and the possible dangers connected therewith.   It has, however, been a matter for the authorities.

They, I take it, have not been indifferent in the matter ; and if, as I am given to understand is the case, considerable care has been taken in the matter of supervising, restricting, and even prohibiting the circulation outside of the United Kingdom of certain so-called occult literature, then the authorities must have felt there was something to be considered.

Spiritism is one of those illogical, emotional crazes which collects around it the loose human ends and mentally crooked sticks of other weak-kneed isms, such as Conchyism and Pacificism— well-meaning, maybe, in the main, but certainly not over wise, exact, or ardently patriotic.

Folk of this mental calibre will do lots of irregular things so long as the doing of them squares with what they consider to be their conscience or is attuned to their emotional vagaries.

Visitors from that other world, which provides a good living for professional earthly practitioners and a mild mental excitement and comforting physical emotions for illogical humans, are drawn presumably from all nations, and, in the general mix up, individual patriotism is scarcely a dominant feature.

The sign-seeker, out for a sign, would welcome a message from any spirit, of no matter what nationality. What his nationality might have been previous to his translation to the celestial sphere would not be a matter for consideration. Whilst a stern, parental Government prohibits delegates in the flesh from meeting enemy envoys at Stockholm, Berne, or any other neutral meeting place, the passportless delegates can come at will from the other world and exchange views with sympathetic mortals with whom they desire to be in communion.

So the most case-hardened, unrepentant enemy spirit can manifest to our pacifists, exchanging views entirely in accord with their own, which, with the spiritual backing behind them, will spread like wildfire amongst the votaries of the spiritistic cult having similar inclinations or holding similar views.

Surely a most fruitful field for the Unseen Hand to till !

And we take infinite pains and go to untold expense in the matter of a war-aims propaganda amongst the hard-working, hard-thinking elements of the population in order to combat the insidious poison of the pacifist movement, whilst this sort of thing, far more subtle, and consequently far less apparent, yet, maybe, more dangerous, goes on unmolested in our midst.

The enemy has ever been fond of using art, science, and public characters for its purpose. The way that fascinating Dutch Batavian dancer, who a short time back met her death as a spy at the hands of the French military authorities, was manipulated by her German paymasters for German ends will be fresh in the memory of my readers. With *artistes* of this type and temperament the enemy has worked extensively, and, from his point of view, with highly successful results.

Years ago there was a Russian princess who was in the pay of Germany for political purposes. She was known to the outside world as a snake-charmer, and, following her ostensible profession, she went everywhere, and into the best society too, collecting much information, and generally aiding the schemes of her political employers.

She was a weird, fascinating creature ; and as it happened that I was enabled to render her at one time a little service, she by degrees unfolded her life-story to me. And what a strange, mysterious story it was, and what an intense human document ! It is too long a story to tell here, but one day I shall relate it.

It was the personal magnetism of this snake princess, and the weird fascination surrounding her vocation, that made her so useful to the Germans for their purposes. In her way she did work equal to that of the mystic Rasputin.

I have already pointed out how German

diplomacy manipulated the mysticism associated
with Abdul Hamid. It, from the point of
German diplomacy, was a good card to play,
and no opportunity is missed of playing a similar
card with advantage. There is so much crass
stupidity, so much illogicality and weakness of
purpose, associated with the dabblers in the
occult, that they unsuspectingly dance to the tune
set them by those who know how to touch the
right chord. From gathering useful information
through their fatuous gabble and making valuable deductions from their queries, to moulding
them, in their weak-kneedness, to advance ideas
suitable for their purpose, the enemy, I fear,
will have struck oil in playing the Unseen Hand
in the coteries obsessed by the mania of getting
in touch with the Unseen World.

An American authority, who has given a close
study to the question, states that the world is
" literally a-crawl " with spies of Central Europe.
These spies, it should be clearly understood, are
not confined to German-born subjects. They are
recruited from all nationalities, and work from
different motives and for widely different rewards.
Some are patriots, and their sense of patriotism
finds gratification in carrying out schemes they
think may be of service to their country, no
matter how devious the methods employed.
Others are out for an ultimate political or commercial "pull," and there is very little unblemished
patriotism about their operations. Then there
are those who seek for social advantages, with an
eye to decorations that a grateful Kaiser may feel

disposed to bestow upon them. The common, or garden, secret agents, of both sexes and of varied nationalities, who are paid in hard cash for their work, according to its estimated value, are a numerous tribe ; but they are not so dangerous as those workers in the enemy's interests who are more highly placed and work from different motives, and are all the more likely to carry on unsuspected.

Our Home Secretary also draws attention to the fact that the spies in Germany's interests are not confined to those of enemy origin, but are to be found amongst neutrals of nearly all countries. So we have Bolos at work in England—Bolos in finance, politics, and society ; but the possibility of a Bolo in spiritism, apparently, has not come within the Boloism reckoning. It seems to me, however, to offer a phase of possible evil requiring careful watching and following up.

Bolo himself, I believe, is a bit of a mystic, with a belief that—in the Eastern way—he can read, with a stick in the sand, the riddle of life. I have frequently seen the past and the present read in this fashion, with more or less accuracy. But shots at the future have been by no means so successful.

I wonder if Bolo has read correctly his own future ?

CHAPTER XI

MYSTIC ODDS AND ENDS

So far as possible I have dealt with the various phases of the so-called occult in chapters to which they would appear to have special application, but there remain over little sidelights—odds and ends, as it were—which do not directly fit in with any one of these descriptive titles. Indeed, there is really no end to the instances which runners after the occult are for ever bringing up for one's refutation or confusion. Each man's personal experience is a law unto itself; and to throw light upon the darkness of his perplexity, or to disprove the erroneousness of his conclusions, carries neither weight nor conviction with others who hug their superstitious fallacies with a kindred tenacity. Life in this world is too short to permit of a reasoned explanation being given of every phase of supernaturalism with which the more or less impressionable person one comes in contact with is for the moment obsessed. I will content myself, therefore, with just a few instances which have come under my personal attention, and which, in my opinion, seem to call more than others for particular notice.

In the early days of my investigations into the occult I was brought much in contact with a young Irishman, who afterwards gained considerable distinction at the criminal bar. He had a somewhat romantic temperament, with, at times, a dreamy mental outlook on life ; but, ordinarily, he was level-headed, with close reasoning powers, and his knowledge of human nature was quite considerable, and, in the main, accurate. Whilst laughing at the claims of spiritualists, describing the manifestations upon which they based their belief in another world as mostly noisy and altogether non-celestial, he professed a belief in phenomena which could alone be the outcome of occult agency or some mysterious force of which no satisfactory explanation, so far, was forthcoming. He had, he claimed, experienced the outcome of this mysterious force, and had witnessed demonstrations so contrary to the recognised laws of nature that he was bound to believe in the reality of occult agencies. A learned Indian who had been reading with him had caused phenomena to be produced that baffled all explanation on any other basis. For instance, a dagger held in his hand over a bowl would gradually lose its rigidity and become as pliable in his hands as putty, eventually dissolving into an impalpable nothingness. He had not only seen this done but had himself commenced obtaining similar results. By this time the Indian student had returned to the " Land of Peacocks," so I was unable to witness a first-hand demonstration ; but again and again my friend promised to personally demonstrate his own powers, so far as they went, in this direction. One evening I visited his chambers in the Middle Temple for this purpose, full of curiosity, tempered, I may add, with just a little healthy scepticism. In the course of the evening the dagger was produced. It was a weird, antique weapon, handsomely chased with quaint figures and symbols. With it, I was told, a murder had quite recently been committed out in the Far East, and I don't think one would have been casting too severe a reflection upon its character by crediting it with more than one little peculiarity of this kind. It was a weapon made to kill, and, in the hands of one bent on killing, would not, I fancy, have disappointed.

My friend took the dagger and held it over an antique, curiously worked silver bowl containing rose leaves. He raised it upwards and pressed it downwards, moved it this way and that, with many a little fantastic twirl, muttering slowly but earnestly a sort of incantation. I took no hand in the matter, merely sitting still and watching. So far as I could see, no change was taking place in the form or substance of the dagger. But the movements and incantation went on. At length I ventured to ask how the experiment was progressing. My friend paused in his movements, and the far-away look in his eyes died out. There was disappointment in his voice as he replied. This time the oracle wasn't working on the hitherto approved plan. He couldn't quite make it out. Perhaps it was through not having got the words of the invocation quite right. A word missed, wrongly placed, or incorrectly pronounced would make all the difference. And it was not an easy formula to remember and enunciate. To me it was all so much meaningless gibberish, given forth though it was with all earnestness. Finally my friend, on laying down the dagger, explained that he generally obtained the best effects in the stillness of the night, and the hour was yet young. Anxious as I was to meet him in his faith in the miraculous in every way possible, I said that time was no object with me, and, if agreeable to him, I would remain all night to see the thing through. And so we sat for hours smoking countless cigarettes, and refreshing ourselves with spirits of a more visible and potent character than those which were merely *en l'air*, so to speak. And yet, after all, the wonder-working did not come off ; and when I finally left, the weapon was lying on the table in precisely the same condition as when it was first taken up.

Subsequent to this sitting my friend took pains to impress upon me the necessity of having the correct atmosphere in association with such phenomena. He was too sensible to mouth the old tag that my sceptical personality was bound to provide an antagonistic element. It was not my presence but the absence of that of the adept, through whom the marvel was originally produced, that was the cause of the failure. When it had come off with him alone he had felt the astral presence of the adept, which, in his opinion,

accounted for the result, for not for a single
moment did he claim for himself occult powers
capable of working wonders of this character.
This adept, he informed me, had assured him of
his ability to project at will his astral presence.
That this projection on various occasions had
taken place he was convinced, as he not only had
felt the presence but had seen it. At this I began
to ask myself if he had not seen the astral form
in much the same way as he had seen the gradual
dematerialisation of the murderous weapon over
which he had made the weird chant the previous
evening. But he was so terribly in earnest over
the matter that I really did not like to express
the full extent of my scepticism. I, however,
begged of him to furnish me with a further
sitting, in the hope of securing the astral form's
attendance. This further sitting was accorded
me. We began at a later hour than on the
previous occasion and at a moment when my
friend said he felt the influence of the astral
presence—the same movements with the dagger,
the same gibberish, and the far-away look in the
eyes, but, so far as I could judge, no perceptible
change in the weapon held above the bowl. Yet
my legal friend declared he felt the change occurring ; " And," said he, " you see the form of the
adept there opposite me ? " And he stared with
a sort of ecstatic satisfaction into the corner of the
room on my right. " See," said he : " it is only
a blue outline, the rest is as a cloud." I followed
his eyes, but I could discern neither blue outline
nor astral shadow. The only cloudy substance in

14

the room apparent to me was the outcome of tobacco smoke. My companion thought me blind. My failure to see what he saw arose from a lack of the highly-attuned imagination by which he was himself influenced. This lack of imagination, I fear, cuts off many of those other-world wonders so distinct to those who possess it.

I did not attend any more dagger-dissolving sittings ; but my friend, to the day of his death, I am sure, felt convinced that the phenomenon had actually occurred in the manner and under the conditions described. So be it !

. . . . . .

The possibility of this astral-form projection is firmly believed in by many who have a leaning towards Eastern occultism. Personally, I have never seen an astral form, although on various occasions I have known adepts for whom this projective art, amongst other mystic gifts, has been claimed. Moreover, amongst my own personal acquaintances there have been those who have expressed the belief that I myself must surely possess a similar power or gift, or whatever goes to make up the force necessary to separate the spiritual from the material of one's earthly composition, and frequently I have been asked to will that my astral self should appear to such and such a person at such and such a place. More than once I have tried the experiment, willing with all my might, thinking with an intensity that begat severe headaches. In accordance, moreover, with the rules laid down in connection with the subject, I have, for the purpose of obtaining the desired result, fasted and been generally ever so good ; but not once have I been conscious of having effected the spiritual separation from the material, although I have been assured that my astral presence has been felt at the time I was putting the projection to the test. But, alas ! beyond the mere assurance that my astral presence had been felt, what proof was there of such projection having taken place ? The statement of those to whom the alleged visit was made would be based upon expectation and the fulfilment of a desire. Outside of this, what other proof ? Now, if the one to whom my astral form had appeared had, for instance, cut off a lock of hair and retained it as a memento of the visit, that, at least, would have been something substantial in the direction of evidence.

The only occasions when I have had seemingly personal evidence of any passing dematerialisation of myself have been during a severe bout of malarial fever, when, lying on bed or couch with an abnormally high temperature, I have watched my head leave the trunk and go bumping around the room, the knocks received by the astral head being felt by the burning material head still remaining on the pillow.

For the purposes of romance one may make use of astral forms ; indeed, in my little shocker, *A Fatal Affinity*, I made extensive use of a creation of this character. But, so far, according to my personal experience, the evidence is all against their having any being in this everyday world of ours.

That one may be able to influence another at

a distance is not improbable; indeed, under certain conditions it possesses the elements of possibility. The person influenced must, however, desire to be influenced, and must know that the impressionist at that particular moment is seeking to establish that influence. It is not enough for one to wish and think with all his might. Thought and wishes will not travel on Marconi-like electric waves, and the thinker and would-be receiver of them would have no proof of their receipt outside of their own anticipations. The impression in such matters comes from within, and not from without; and one may safely say that it is this inner feeling which, in the case of astral forms, is mistaken for outward presence.

The feminine temperament is more ripe to feel impressions of this kind than the masculine, and the more ready to make false deductions therefrom. Sentiment and temperament are closely allied to the mystic.

A very dear lady of my acquaintance, who has decidedly mystic leanings, strengthened by a long residence in the East, is strongly of opinion that she and I met in some form or other in the dim ages of the past. The opinion, or the feeling, as she puts it, came to her the first time we met, gathering conviction with further association. For my part, I, who have no evidence what any pre-existence of mine might have done in the past, or whom it may have known, can only say that the affinity of the present may very well preserve the affinity of a past, provided such a past permitted of a previous acquaintance.

Feelings and beliefs of this kind are very common, and amongst those, too, who know nothing about the reincarnation theory.

How often have I heard people say that they feel, after a first meeting, as if they had really known this or that person before ; and how very common is the expression, " We seem to have known each other all our lives," although the knowledge in reality may have been of but short duration ! The affinity of the present is prone to draw upon the may-have-been of the unknown past. There is some naturalness about this, and some pleasure too. Were the assumption not so pleasant, it, I take it, would not be so readily assumed.

All this sort of thing, of course, is based upon mere assumption. For who can say what and who we were in the dim ages of the past— provided, indeed, we had any previous existence at all ?

From the standpoint of pure reasonableness on an evolutionary basis the theory of spiritual reincarnation may well be said to be ahead of spiritism. For, with the spiritistic creed, often we, in spirit form, may serve to provide some fraudulent medium with funds and fail to furnish those that are nearest and dearest to us with absolute proof of that other world to which it is claimed we have been translated.

Against this reincarnation theory stands the protest that one term of earthly tribulation is enough for any mortal to undergo. Earthly tribulation, however, is a matter for the body

rather than the spirit.   The Old Ones of ancient
Egypt held that Thoth weighed the souls and
not the bodies of those who passed from earth
to the Judgment Seat.   The physical remains of
those appearing for judgment lay wrapped up in
their mummy-clothes where they had been deposited, and what was found wanting in the
spiritual part when it was placed upon the scales
was entered up against it.   Earthly judgment
had already sat upon the transgressions of the
body, and the lengthy screed describing the many
virtues of the deceased placed with the mummy
was for human consumption only.   The findings
of the God of Truth were a lasting record, and
were in most cases possibly greatly at variance
with the earthly estimate in which the departed
had been held.   Presumably Thoth, in weighing
the soul when released from another earthly shell,
noted any improvement or deterioration it may
have shown since the last weighing, just as the
earthly case, duly mummified, would have its
earthly record chronicled as usual.   That, surely,
is as much as any mortal or spirit can expect !

.   .   .   .   .   .

Apropos of astral projection, a mystic friend of
mine, who has travelled much, and has a knowledge of many peoples and their languages, holds
very pronounced views in connection with projection possibilities.   He does not go the length
of asserting that it is possible to appear astrally
in one place whilst remaining *in propria persona*
in another.   But he emphatically asserts his ability

to transport an intelligible message at a distance
to anyone *en rapport* with him. This, I gather,
is not so much the outcome of occult powers as
the result of concentrated thought and will power.
He claims to have first acquired the habit of conveying such messages whilst in Thibet, and he
has furnished me with numerous instances of the
success he has achieved in this direction. I have
no means of testing the accuracy of his statements,
and, in the absence of such a test, I must content
myself with accepting them as related for just
what they may be worth. But, in my own case,
I can speak with some definiteness. My friend,
from the first, was of opinion that by temperament
and affinity of thought I was an ideal subject for
such transmission, and begged me to put the
matter to the test. I willingly assented, and
undertook to conform to the conditions he might
lay down.

They were to the effect that on retiring to bed
I should concentrate my entire thought upon receiving a message he would cause to be sent me.
Whilst doing this I, with wide-open eyes, was to
gaze into the darkness of the room for the sign.
It would come in the shape of a faint blue circle,
and within the circle would appear the message.
Knowing the man's linguistic versatility, I asked
him if the words would be in a language I could
understand, and if it would be written from left
to right or from right to left. He thought a
moment, and then said it would be in a language I could understand, and the writing would
run from left to right. The suggestion inter-

ested me not a little, and I rigidly obeyed the
instructions laid down. How I gazed into the
darkness of my bedroom! how I lay still waiting
and hoping for the appearance of that blue circle,
thinking hard all the while! The minutes went
by and the hours, until it was past the appointed
time when the message was to reach me. Still
I kept my thoughts concentrated upon the hope
that it would at length be made visible to me. . . .
A flash of blue across the window, penetrating for
an instant the drawn curtains! Was that the fore-
runner of the mystic circle? No, it was but the
tail-end of a searchlight. Quite an old acquaintance these raid nights! It was, however, the
only blue light I was to see that night. A short
time afterwards the night's stillness was broken
by exploding shrapnel and the thud of falling
bombs. A raid was in full swing.

In that raid my astrally-conveyed message
must have lost its way; or maybe it omitted to
take shelter, and came to grief through running
its head against shells of purely mundane origin!
Anyway, it failed to reach me, and I had all
my waiting and watching for nothing. It was
discouraging, but I was willing to admit that
the raid might have upset its arrangements, and
that it might fairly claim to have not had a fair
sporting chance. My mystic friend, when I saw
him the following morning, adopted this view.
But, as I pointed out, the raid, so far as my
mental concentration was concerned, did not com-
mence for an hour or two after the time agreed
upon for the receipt of the astral message. To

this he replied, with an air of some superiority, that as an outcome of the raid the atmospheric conditions would probably be disturbed for some time previous to the actual overhead firing ; and, under such disturbed and unexpected atmospheric conditions, difficulties would be placed in the way of the proper conveyance of a message of this character. My friend is an electrical and mining engineer as well as a linguist of mystic inclinations, and he advanced a number of scientific reasons for the failure of the test under the conditions then prevailing. " Leave it at that," was my reply. But, being anxious to give the test a fair trial, I asked how long it might be following the raid before suitable conditions might with certainty be anticipated. He explained that the conditions generally were most favourable during full moon. As this period, however, is the one considered most favourable by the raiders, I suggested that we should wait a while, till, say, the birth of the new moon. To this he assented. Finally, he agreed upon a night when another attempt should be made to convey the message to me.

Again I lay awake and thought and stared ; but there came no blue circle, no writing therein. And there was no raid that night, nothing, so far as I knew, to disturb the atmospheric conditions so dear to occultly-conveyed messages of this character. Frankly, I was greatly disappointed. It was one of those convincing objective signs for which I had been seeking, and the certainty of which had been assured me. All my friend could say in explanation of the failure was that the fault lay with me. He had placed himself *en rapport* with me, and had willed the message, but that I had lacked the requisite mental concentration, or had let other outside thoughts usurp the place of the central idea.

I promptly negatived this explanation. Concentration of thought is a matter which I feel I can carry out with some degree of perfection. Years of effort have made it all the easier for me. The explanation of the failure of the test was, therefore, not to be found in this direction. I, moreover, was in no way antagonistic to the reception of such a message as my mystic friend felt he was able to convey. On the contrary, I was really quite desirous of its success, and, accordingly, was disappointed at its failure to materialise. My friend either overestimated his powers in this direction, or miscalculated my suitability from the point of affinity to be the recipient of messages of this character. We will leave it at that.

He assured me, however, that sooner or later he would get a message through to me, maybe when I least expected it, as it was impossible to lay down hard-and-fast rules in matters of this kind. He instanced the case of a man to whom he had sent a message from Thibet. This man at the time was somewhere in Southern China, and he had not heard whether the message had made itself known. The circumstance, he assured me, had been forgotten until, some years afterwards, happening to meet the man to whom the communication had been made, it was suddenly recalled. And the man, he went on, began with describing how the message became visible to him, and then repeated the words making up the message, words which in themselves were at the time meaningless to him.

After this there is hope in my case too. When the message originally sent me has grown tired of wandering aimlessly around, it may elect to pay me a visit for my information and conviction. It may happen also that further messages which my friend promises to flash me may find me at the moment more *en rapport* with the sender, and at the same time will enjoy those atmospheric conditions which would appear to constitute an element to success !

.   .   .   .   .   .

I have already pointed out how people have credited me with gifts to which I lay no claim, and assume I must have powers which—consciously at least—I certainly do not possess. This is unavoidable, and one gets used to being misunderstood. But it is a horse of another colour when people, claiming to be my pupils, indulge in mysticisms altogether foreign to my practices and antagonistic to my contentions. I could cite countless instances of this kind—diverting and otherwise. One of the most diverting is contained in a story told by Lord Shaughnessy, the President of the Canadian Pacific Railway. And how well he tells it !

His predecessor in office was Sir William van Horne, with whom in my earlier visits to Canada

I was brought much in contact, especially in connection with literary work associated with Canada, on which I was then engaged. Sir William was interested also in my psychological work, and, on my leaving Canada, claimed that my mantle had fallen upon his shoulders. But, it goes without saying, the master was not in it with the pupil, who professed to be able to do what certainly was quite beyond me to accomplish. A very astute man was Sir William, and he worked his little mind-reading fakes with considerable skill and effect, and afforded his associates no little bewildering amusement.

One day, according to Lord Shaughnessy, Sir William with other C.P.R. directors was travelling on the official car from Ottawa to Montreal, when the ex-President gave the company a display of his mind-reading powers.

" Say, Van," said one of the company, " you seem to be in such good trim this evening that you might read the number of my watch."

" I guess you're too late this evening," replied Van Horne, assuming an appropriate weary and worn-out expression. " I'm tired out now. Another time with pleasure." So the test was left for that other time. It came a week or so later, when the same company was making another journey in the official car. Again there were more mind-reading illustrations, and the mind-reader was reminded about telling the number of the watch.

" I guess I can fix that little matter up now," said van Horne, " as I am feeling in just the mood for it.   So fetch out your watch, and let me have a shot at it."

The watch was produced, and the mind-reader, with an appropriate far-away look in his eyes, placed it to his forehead.   Slowly he gave the number, describing the last figure as being blurred and difficult to decipher.

" Well, how's that ? " he asked with an air of triumph.

" Wonderful," said the owner of the watch ; " and the description of the blurred last figure is a masterpiece.   But, Van, your description covers the watch I carried last week.   *This is another one* I'm wearing for the first time." Tableau !

　　·　　　·　　　·　　　·　　　·　　　·

To have attributed to you powers which you in no way possess, however flattering it may be to the Old Adam of vanity which has its place in the composition of most men, is calculated to absorb a good deal of one's time, and to exhaust most of one's patience.   I have had people seek me out with an attitude that was intensely mystic, merely to gratify a momentary whim.   Once, in Paris, a very distinguished and charming lady simply haunted my hotel in her efforts to find me disengaged and willing to grant her an interview.   She would leave no message and would not put her query in writing.   The matter in question was of too delicate and im-portant a character to reach me second-hand. It had to be put to me personally—and alone. At last chance favoured her, and she succeeded

in catching me when I was alone and disengaged.
I shall never forget the intensity with which she
put her query into words, and the longing look
in her eyes as she awaited my reply.   And all it
amounted to after all was, would I find her lost
Planchette ?   Great stress was laid upon the fact
that Planchette was a "lady dog," and had a
curly tail.   Every effort had been made to discover the whereabouts of the missing pet.   She
had exhausted all the usual channels, and had had
recourse to clairvoyantes without avail, so in her
despair she had come to me.   Money was no
object, and she would not be lacking in gratitude.
She was a very graceful, charming lady, and
gratitude from her in itself would have been a
rich reward.   But, alas for her peace of mind !
I had to tell her that the mission of finding lost
dogs in either the "lady" or "gentleman"
category and with or without curly tails was
not mine.   I advised her to stick to her mystic
guides, who, even if they did not succeed in
finding the missing Planchette, would certainly
supply her with encouraging and consoling information so long as she was ready to pay for it.

The lady left me, I fear, in something
approaching a "pet," and, in her disappointment, was disposed to consider me more of an
unsympathetic brute than an all-discerning seer.

In Madrid a young lady, noted for her beauty
and musical gifts, whom I had met on several
occasions at the British Embassy, paid me a visit
in company with her duenna in order to ascertain
something very near what, I presume, she would

have termed her heart. The stately duenna waited discreetly in the anteroom whilst my fascinating visitor, with impassioned volubility, declared the object of her visit. It was just this : Two young bloods of Madrid were very much in love with her. On family grounds one was as acceptable as the other, and, personally, she really had no preference. She could not marry both, but, eventually, would surely marry one of them —but which ? Would I advise her ? Would I make the choice for her ? Alas ! what had I to do with other people's little love affairs ? And what man has yet been born who could safely and wisely take upon himself such a momentous decision ? Obviously I promptly declined the rôle cast for me. But she resented my refusal with the prettiest possible display of petulance. I explained that in my country when in doubt we frequently tossed for it, letting the spin of the coin determine our decision. It, I added, would possibly collide with her conception of things to toss a coin with " Heads—José ; tails —Juan." She agreed that it would not be a convincing decision. It, to tell the truth, was much too matter-of-fact for her romantic disposition. There is chance, but precious little sentiment, associated with the tossing of a coin. Finally, I suggested that as she was uncertain in her choice, and as, presumably, it didn't really matter much either way who was the successful suitor, she should let Fate or chance decide for her. This suggestion made a direct appeal to her sentimentality. And she left me determined to accept the one—whether José or Juan—she happened first to meet after departing from my hotel. As I left Madrid the next day, I was at that time unacquainted with what chance had decided for Clarita. Indeed, I have never had the pleasure of since seeing the lady and receiving her congratulations or reproaches which she surely would have meted out to me, deservedly or otherwise.

But in the years to follow I was to hear again of Clarita and her love affairs. My Ambassador, who had been her host in Madrid, had become Ambassador at Constantinople. At the Embassy one day the topic of conversation turned upon events in the Spanish capital. Said his Excellency to me, with mock severity :

"That, my friend, was an unfortunate choice of yours about Clarita."

"How so, sir ? "

"Oh, didn't you hear? Well, after leaving you, the first man she met happened to be Juan ; and, having let chance decide for her, she favoured that worthy young man in preference to all others —and, finally, married him. And what an unhappy marriage it turned out to be ! The dear Clarita, I am afraid, blames you and not her own choice, as if you had anything to do with regulating Fate's chance meeting. It is just possible that if it had been the other way about, and Clarita had first met José instead of Juan, the marriage might have been equally unfortunate, and you would have been blamed all the same. That is woman's way."

"And José, sir?"

"Oh, he, it was said, was searching for you with a knife or something unpleasantly aggressive, as it had got about that Clarita in her choice had acted upon a suggestion you had made her. Woman-like, she didn't keep the suggestion to herself. She told everyone—including myself—how she was in Fate's hands. That, again, is woman's way. Now you will see, *mon ami*, what comes of giving women advice in connection with their love affairs: an unhappy wife, a fearfully jealous husband, and an impetuous, indiscreet lover. And divorce is so difficult in Spain!"

Since then, as becomes a penitent, I for my sins have taken unto sackcloth and ashes—an unbecoming and uncomfortable garb when worn even merely metaphorically.

. . . . . .

Boulanger, of whom I saw a good deal in Paris in the height of his popularity, and later in exile in London, had mystic instincts. He was decidedly of opinion that he was the "Man of Destiny"; and he, I am afraid, was disappointed at my inability to prophesy that future for him which his ambition and instincts had caused him to map out for himself. He was a man who said little but who thought a good deal, and, being of an emotional disposition, was apt to let his emotions get the better of him, frequently giving himself away without really knowing it. M. de Blowitz, the Paris correspondent of the

Times, took occasion to telegraph an account of a séance I had had with *le brav' général* which teemed with indiscretions, mostly, I should say, having their origin in the fertile imagination of M. de Blowitz himself. It did Boulanger a bad turn, but maybe, as matters eventuated, France a good one.

Le brav' général stood at that time for all that France aspired to in the direction of *revanche*. And when it became known that the dominant thought in his mind as my " subject " was Stuttgart as the objective of an imaginary campaign, the idea was received with acclamation, although, after all, it was purely a phantasy, and the circumstance was not intended for publication and in no case to be taken seriously.

It is at least a somewhat curious circumstance that the Würtemberg capital should in these days of actual warfare have been the objective of French attack, but by an arm of warfare undreamt of in Boulanger's time.

About the time Boulanger was looking to me for psychic confirmation of his mystic ideas, a clairvoyante, who had read his hand, told him that he ran the risk of coming to grief through a woman. But at this he had only smiled. Boulanger had too great a faith in his star, and, as a confirmed ladies' man, too much confidence in himself where the fair sex was concerned, to give the prophecy serious consideration. And yet a woman was his undoing ; and anyone who saw his infatuation for the woman who brought it about, and the extraordinary influence she was gradually but surely establishing over him, need not have had even the faintest claim to prophetic powers to have concluded what the inevitable end would be unless a breach occurred.

Boulanger was a man of some parts, and he possessed a certain personal magnetism that was quite attractive, but he lacked grip and determination. He allowed himself to be run instead of dictating how others should be run. The one man around Boulanger who best understood him was Count Dillon. Had he strictly followed his advice, and at the same time broken with Madame de Bonnemain, there might have been a different end from the sadly tragic one enacted over that grave in Brussels.

.   .   .   .   .   .

Arabi was another of life's failures who had mystic instincts, and whose vaulting ambition was spurred by an occult forecast. He had been told by one of those weird fortune-tellers, so numerous in his native land, that a great future was in store for him as a sort of political mahdi. In his dull way he began to believe in his star, and to work out the methods of reaching the goal foreshadowed in the prophecy. The outcome of his political activities is ancient history.

I visited Arabi when he was in exile in Ceylon. A more subdued, ambitionless, patriotic firebrand it would be impossible to imagine. True, the humid climate of the island did not suit Arabi, but it did not altogether account for the man's utter spiritlessness.

He was anxious for me to give him some illustrations of thought-reading, such as I had demonstrated with the Khedive in Cairo. I did so, and successfully too. But Arabi was anything but a good "subject." He was keen on my telling him what the future had in store for him. I explained that no man could say what the future would bring forth, that I could read only what a man himself knew, and, as he himself did not know about his own future, there was not furnished a readable proposition. His one hope, I gathered, was to go back to Egypt, to die if not to live. He was now a man of peace, without ambition, and from whom nothing more need be feared.

I came to the conclusion that the subdued Arabi's estimate of himself was correct, and that all the prophecy nonsense had been knocked out of him, and I wrote home accordingly.

I would mention that I looked in on Arabi in Ceylon from an extended visit to India, during which I had been the bearer of a congratulatory message from the Khedive Tewfyk to Lord Dufferin on his appointment as Viceroy. Lord Dufferin suggested that it would be quite interesting to see what I made of Arabi psychologically.

In connection with this message, when I next visited Egypt—Tewfyk Pasha had joined his fathers, and his son Abbas reigned in his place— his Highness was good enough to show me some attention, and, carrying out what appeared to have been the wishes of his father, conferred upon me the Commandership of the Medjideh, and created me a Bey.

In connection with my presentation to Abbas on my arrival at Cairo I found awaiting me at my hotel a message from a high official at the Abdin Palace saying that his Highness would be pleased to receive me the next day at noon. Upon this I went to Lord Cromer and asked him if, as a British subject, my presentation should, as in the case with the Khedive Tewfyk, come through him. Lord Cromer at once replied that it was better to let the matter go through in the way his Highness apparently desired it. In fact, he pointed out that he wished it that way too, adding, I should in all probability get closer to the real thoughts of the Khedive if brought in touch with him unofficially. "And," he added, "one would much like to know his real thoughts. He certainly is the most perplexing psychological study I have ever come across." From time to time, subsequent to this, I gave Lord Cromer accounts of my reading of his Highness. About this time, I would add, the relations between the young Khedive and Lord Cromer were somewhat strained. His Highness entered upon his position as Khedive in much the same way as a spoiled child enters into possession of a new toy—a toy to be done with just as the momentary whim may take him. Verily, he was hall-marked with the petulancy of the spoiled child. Vienna society had done its best to spoil him, and had succeeded beyond, maybe, its expectations. In addition, his associa-

tions with the most aristocratic Court in Europe
had instilled in him autocratic notions which
did not go well in Egypt, following so closely
the liberal-minded ideas of his father. In temperament and ambition his Highness, I was
assured, more closely resembled Abbas I. than
any other member of the Khedivial family who
had preceded him.

I particularly noticed that his Highness,
although he spoke English perfectly, preferred
to speak in German ; and he certainly thought
in that language, even when he was conversing
in English.

I must say that I found Abbas an exceedingly
interesting " subject." He too appeared to take
an interest in me, not on account of my being
British, but as a man who had travelled and had
received some attention at the Courts upon which
he would much have liked to model his own.
Abbas certainly did not understand the psychology
of the English. The bad taste only too frequently
displayed by a certain class of Cook's tourists he
had come to accept as typical of the English
nation ; and he complained to me personally of
the " side " of these bumptious, moneyed non-
descripts, who flaunted it at the fashionable hotels,
and chipped mementoes off Sphinx and Pyramids.
" They give themselves the air of conquerors,"
he concluded, with much bitterness. And at
the back of his head, I fancy, there became a
fixed idea that Lord Cromer not only represented
the British nation with all its dominating influences, but that he was the wood itself out of

which these objectionable types which so aroused his Highness' ire were actually cut. The two men eventually understood each other better, but there was a pretty long spell of give-and-take before this was arrived at. Abbas was too prone to get the bit between his teeth ready for a bolt ; and Lord Cromer, knowing his super-sensitive nature, had to drive with an exceedingly careful hand.

One thing his Highness resented above all others was the official attitude adopted towards a little liaison of his with an attractive young lady he brought with him from Vienna. With that goody-goodiness which so distinguishes us, we lifted our official eyebrows and pursed our official lips in an attitude of censorious superiority over the matter. And, after all, what had Abbas' little love affairs to do with us—officially ? He never could understand that it was just the English way—this outstanding moral superiority over every other nation under the sun. He took it as another instance of being sat upon and kept under. His proud and impatient spirit revolted ; and one may safely assume that the young lady in question missed no opportunity of fanning the flame of discontent and adding fuel to his grow-ing hatred of all things English. I wonder if this Viennese light-o'-love had a political part to play after all ? Was it affection that brought her from the Austrian capital to Cairo, or something with a deeper-lying object ? It cannot be said that the Khedive at that time was pro-German, although Austria—as distinct from Germany—

was undoubtedly his "spiritual home." There
were Germans, however, in Cairo who were
talking much and thinking more, and the most
prominent and active amongst them was the
notorious Dr Carl Peters. Of all the men I
have ever met, Peters stands first in his un-
disguised anti-British sentiments. The origin of
this feeling it was not difficult to discover. It
had, I should say, its being in jealousy. Peters had
a petty, jealous nature, and it was gall and worm-
wood to him to see what Great Britain had
accomplished as a world Power, and how well
received was a Britisher who had done anything
for his country, wherever he might go. One
night at Cairo I was invited to a little festive
gathering composed mostly of Germans of note.
It was purely a social affair, and had not the remotest connection with anything political ; but
on the chairman proposing my health in a com-
plimentary little speech in excellent English, Dr
Carl Peters got up and vigorously protested
against the use of a language foreign to the
company when German—especially as I understood it—was the proper language to use. "We
hear quite enough English wherever we go in
Egypt without having it drummed into our ears
here," he added, as he sat down in high dudgeon.
There were loud protests ; and when I explained
that the sincerity of the welcome had been brought
all the more clearly home to me through being
so perfectly expressed in a language which I best
understood, the approving shouts of the company
made the militant Peters look very small indeed.

The following night there was a *bal masqué* at the Opera House, which Peters excused himself from attending. An American visitor of my acquaintance suspected that an intrigue with "madam" covered the excuse, and on the way to the Opera House asked me, after unburdening himself as to the suspicions that were troubling him, to " stand by him." My acquaintance was a reckless, shoot-at-sight sort of man ; and as I had no wish to see blood spilt over one who, in my opinion, was scarcely worth risking life or reputation for, I willingly assented, determining to take every precaution against a fatal encounter. After a brief stay at the ball the American took me aside. " I'm ready," he said ; " will you come ? " He slipped unnoticed from the crowd, and, keeping close in touch with him, I followed him quickly to our hotel. At the entrance he significantly touched his pocket. I saw the butt-end of a revolver sticking out. As he mounted the stairs I managed to relieve him of that weapon. As events turned out, the revolver would not have come into play that night. The gallant doctor had met with an accident, badly breaking his leg, and was confined to his room, which he was unable to leave for weeks after M. et Madame had returned to Yurrup.

Dr Peters, amongst other phantasies in connection with colonial exploration, was obsessed with the idea that he had discovered the veritable Land of Ophir ; and, what doubtless was of even greater personal satisfaction to him, succeeded in getting his credulous countrymen to swallow this belief to the extent of buying shares in companies he formed for the purpose of exploiting his discoveries.

According to Peters, mystic influences, in which wild and untamed monkeys took a part, guided him in his finds. Those hairy denizens of the wilds would come down to the river bank in the morning and talk with him, and point out where to prospect. "They were good friends of mine," Peters once assured me. About, I should say, the only "good friends" Dr Carl Peters ever made in German East Africa the whole time he was there.

.   .   .   .   .   .

Egyptian magic of to-day is but a poor sort of thing as compared with that ruling in the land at the time of the Pharaohs. Then, one is forced to conclude, it is only too true that the magicians in high places—as with the seers of our own later day—resorted to trickery, mechanical and otherwise, for their effects. None, in reality, may have possessed supernatural powers ; but the mental and other gifts of some were none the less remarkable, and they achieved results which might well have been considered miraculous. For instance, that famous servant of the gods, I-Em-Hotep, High Priest of Ra, had not only considerable scientific knowledge, but possessed powers of suggestion to a most remarkable extent. Recent discoveries of mine have caused me to write a book around this great man and his times. It is pure romance,

with, however, a background of scientific possibilities. I have already found a title for it—
The Servant of the Master—and it will be my next publication.

To-day in Egypt one has to content oneself with the mental and physical hysterics of dancing dervishes and the speculative inaccuracies of fortune-tellers—readers of the hand or through signs drawn in the sands.

I have in mind a prominent sign-reader and fortune-teller of this class who, whilst getting fairly near to facts covering the past and present, made—as events turned out—woefully bad hits with respect to the future.   His name was Abdul, and he did very well out of visitors with curiosity to be satisfied.   In later years he pitched his tent in Paris and London.   Here the law bade him pack it up and make tracks for a more suitable site.   At the first consultation with Abdul there were three ladies with me—one English and two French.   At the English lady he shook his head.   He could make nothing of her.   This I put down to her obvious matter-of-factness.   But with the French ladies the seer was exceedingly voluble, and described the past, present, and future of each without the slightest hesitation.   One was never to get married or have children, but was to go on her "lonely," as it were, the world over in single blessedness.   But the other was to marry late in life, and quite an old man at that.   And she was to have one child —a boy.   But he in his turn would not marry. When asked why he wouldn't marry, the seer answered that he would not marry because he could not, but why he could not was left un-explained.   Maybe by the time he arrived at marriageable age the stock of marriageable girls would have run out !

In the result, the lady who was to marry late in life is still unmarried, and very much in the sere and yellow leaf of disappointed old maidism ; and, as far as anything is certain in this world, one, I think, can safely assume that no old man will in the end be found coming along to offer her his hand and fortune.

As to the other lady, doomed to feverish travel-ling unrest and unwedded loneliness, she has been more or less a fixture in one place, and the last time I saw her she was walking hand-in-hand with a boy in knickerbockers—her son.

As to myself, I was to experience a spell of varied years of health and prosperity—in periods of seven lean and seven fat.   So far the fat ones have not materialised.   Maybe they are merely waiting till after the war !

The last time I met Abdul was in a West-end café.   He had dropped his white headgear and flowing robes, and was dressed in sombre black —a far less picturesque figure than in the old days.   In the course of conversation I reminded him how much astray his prophecies had gone. He solemnly shook his head, and explained with many gestures that many unforeseen things hap-pened in life to make things otherwise certain become uncertain ; and, with respect to the ladies, he, in his broken English, went on to add, " French ladies verra unsure about marriage and children," which, to his mind, I suppose, sufficiently explained the matter. Asked how he was getting on in London, the seer explained that the London atmosphere was " verra bad " for his work, and that the police were " verra bad men." For latter-day necromancers the police, I am free to admit, are not exactly good. And, generally speaking, it is just as well they are not.

.   .   .   .   .   .

From invoking spirits from the other world to dealing with the shades of the under-world is with certain mentally constituted folk but a short step. Your neurotics and crooked mental sticks are for ever seeking after something un-canny and out of the common, a something that is sour to the palate of the healthy-minded. I have more than once during my travels come across those who have indulged in a little Satanic worship on the quiet. The followers of this form of uncanniness are a furtive set, working mostly in secret and in the dark. In more than one European capital little coteries have been formed who have embraced the devil-worship cult and, within the circle containing the followers thereof, have openly practised certain mysterious devilish rites. The followers have been mostly women, but the chief of the circle has invariably been of the male sex. He generally has managed to work himself up into the belief that he is something exceptionally devilish, and to impress upon the hysterical following that he is a being to be feared as well as obeyed. To obtain from him powers to do as much mischief as possible in this world has, I believe, been the dominating reason with the perverted following for remaining members of the cult. I have been asked to attend a gala-night séance with the chief on his throne and with all the rites in full swing, but I have never had the stomach for such adventure ; and, in any case, I would never have gone alone or without the stoutest dog-whip I could lay my hands on. The dog-whip well laid on is about the only antidote for such blasphemous folly. On one occasion, however, I gave an otherwise highly intelligent and deeply read young man, who had gone over, or was on the verge of going over, to the crazy movement, an hour or so of attention whilst he unfolded his views on the subject. He was of opinion that it was far easier to work evil than good in this world, and that the devil, the chief worker of evil, was the more powerful influence this side of death. Satan, he opined, was ever destructive and never by any chance creative ; but there was one anti-dote against his destructiveness, the secret of which he possessed. He ended by opening a case and fetching from it three peacocks' feathers ; one he placed in each of my hands, passing the other over my brow and tickling me with it behind my ears, reading the while from a black-letter MS. in front of him. It sounded strange in the stillness of that room ; but of the actual meaning of it I had not the remotest idea, as the words were in a language utterly unknown to me. In the end I was declared to be immune against Satanic machinations ; and, at the same time, the offer was made to enrol me as a sort of Grand Master to render equal immunity to others. Now, that young man was not mad in the ordinary acceptance of the term insane, but he was a decidedly queer case, and, without doubt, terribly in earnest. He has passed out of my life, and the mystic peacocks' feathers served as pipe-cleaners, thus doing probably more effective, useful work than that which they were intended to perform.

.   .   .   .   .   .

A phase of the mystic which greatly impressed me the first time I witnessed it. I was very young at the time, and not up to all the little tricks of the trade. It consisted of writing appearing in letters of blood upon the arm of the seer whose hand I was holding. The letters gradually formed themselves, until the whole word was clearly visible and readable, slowly fading and disappearing, leaving the arm perfectly normal again. The mystic, in a second attempt, succeeded in bringing out in a like manner a name and date I *had first written* on a piece of paper, which I afterwards concluded he must have seen or got at in some way unknown to me. Later I was to discover how easy it was to get at what an inquirer might convey to paper. But the writing, how was that managed ? Having got name and date, the next thing was to get the arm to speak. But there was no spiritual agency or

mystic art known to me which would produce
such an effect. The writing had, therefore, to
be impressed on the arm by mundane means.
I commenced writing names and dates on my
own left arm and watching the effect. I made
a sad bungle of it at first. Either the stylus I
used was too pointed and bruised the skin, or
was pressed too deeply and was too visible at the
start. But after some practice, and having at
length adopted a stylus of the right pointedness,
I managed it all right, and was able to reproduce naturally what was alleged to be the outcome of an obliging supernaturalism.

I gave a demonstration to that eminent
physician Sir James Paget, who made some
interesting comments upon the peculiarity of my
skin, the composition of which so well permitted
me to carry out the experiment. It would appear
that differently constituted flesh would not furnish
means for the production of similar results. I
am glad that the writing fades into nothingness,
leaving no after-marks of what has been there;
or my arm, after the illustrations of the mystic
art it has been called upon to furnish, would
indeed be a sight for the gods; and what a police
clue, too, in case one were " wanted " !

. . . . . .

As I say elsewhere, the supernaturalism of the
West does not go with the occultism of the East.
The two things are apart, and my detailed
experiences of Eastern occultism are for another
occasion. But, before closing this chapter, I

may include just one mystic item peculiar to
India.

There was not so long ago a very-much-talked-
of mystic whose marvels, which created almost
a sensation, were the subject of the widest con-
troversy. A distinguished Indian Political of my
acquaintance gave me a description of an incident
which had occurred in his presence, the hang of
which he frankly admitted was beyond him.

There was a little tea-party in the hills to
which he had been invited, but which at the
time he felt he would be unable to attend. But
it so happened that at the last moment he found
himself able to put in an appearance. His
attendance being unexpected, he found on his
arrival they were a cup and saucer short. This
did not, however, in the least disconcert the giver
of the feast, for was not the almost divine mystic
there, and would not she in some way or other
make good the shortcoming? But how? Cups
and saucers were not taken from the air after the
fashion of conjurers' coins ; and even if they were,
who would dare to associate this gifted being with
such vulgarities as mere sleight-of-hand tricks?
No, madam had another and more convincing
way of working the oracle. The usual far-away
look, the familiar gibberish and mystic movements
of the hands, and, lo and behold ! the problem was
solved. An invisible astral form had indicated
where a cup and saucer would be found ready
for use. It was embedded in the solid earth at
their feet. Dig, and they would find. And the
digging commenced, solid undisturbed earth being

removed and cast away until, some distance down, the diggers came upon the articles desired.

"I am convinced," said my friend, "there was a fake somewhere, but where it came in puzzles me. The earth from the surface downwards until we came upon the cup and saucer had been undisturbed, so, obviously, they had not been planted there beforehand. The trickster certainly did his work very cleverly, however he did it."

Knowing something of the way in which these miracles were worked, I put the following questions to him :—

"Were the cup and saucer of the same pattern as the rest of the set ?

"To whom did they belong ?

"And if not the property of the mystic, could she have had previous access to them ? "

The answer to question one was in the affirmative ; and to question two, that the owner was the giver of the tea-party, with whom the mystic was temporarily staying.

My friend also admitted that it would be of considerable indirect advantage to the mystic to have had him present at the gathering, especially if he left it mystified.

"There," I said, "we have the milk in the cocoanut ; and it would be worth getting the little surprise ready in case you, after all, managed to turn up. If you hadn't done so, then probably there would have been nothing doing."

I explained that whilst I was quite ready to accept as perfectly accurate the circumstance as he had related it, yet as it had appeared to me something might have been left out, some trifling thing which would have furnished the desired clue. One thing was quite certain, that the cup and saucer had not been placed there by mahatmaistic influence, but was the work of human hands. Whose ? Now, the mystic had associated with her a very cunning young Indian, who had been very useful in working other miracles ; and if he were with her on the occasion of the tea-party incident, he, in all probability, had a hand in that too. Further examination of the incident put me in touch with the key to the mystery. The tea-party had taken place on a tableland at the edge of a precipitous cliff ; and it struck me that an explanation would be found in the probability of someone having been previously lowered over the cliff, and thus enabled to make a tunnel under the tableland, depositing the cup and saucer at the end of this tunnel, so that lateral digging would go through solid earth until the hidden objects were reached. An examination proved the correctness of this surmise. The little tunnel and the footmarks where the excavator had clung on to the face of the cliff with his toes, after being lowered from a rope made taut on the ground above, were distinctly traceable. The young man who did the trick was the same young man I had in my mind ; and I believe he afterwards owned up to the part he played.

With this, ye mystic odds and ends, adieu !

CHAPTER XII

THE preceding chapters will have shown what my personal experiences in the realms of the mystic have been, what my observations have noted and my examinations discovered. I could have added to them materially, but to have done so would have entailed not a little overlapping and tiresome reiteration. There is a familiar family likeness associated with these so-called occult phenomena, they, more or less, being hewn from one parent piece of wood. I think I have said enough to convince all common-sense, right-thinking people of the purely natural aspect of much that has been erroneously labelled supernatural. I am, however, quite sure that what I have said will not bring conviction to those who are not out to be convinced, and, with not a few, that I shall arouse a condemnation unqualified by the faintest sense of appreciation.

One is up against a strange phase of mentality in dealing with the phantasies to which the out-and-out spiritist is wedded. Instead of being appreciative of any action which serves to lay bare imposture, or to establish beyond cavil the spuriousness of phenomena ascribed to spirit forces, one finds the spiritist adopting an attitude of resentment not unmixed with abuse. This attitude leaves me perfectly calm; but, nevertheless, it is a somewhat absurd one to adopt. Being built that way, the spiritist cannot help himself, I suppose.

I do not accuse every believer in the occult of conscious deception. Far from it. Most emphatically I would say I have no doubt that very many are perfectly sincere and honest in their beliefs, however one may question the correctness of the conclusions arrived at. But alas! they themselves will not admit the possibility of self-deception or erroneous deductions having part in their conclusions.

I do not believe in spirit phenomena, through, in the first place, being of the firm opinion that the natural covers everything associated with them; and, in the second place, that my personal experiences have tended to cement beyond question this conviction.

True, as I have already said, I may have been singularly unfortunate in my experiences, but in such matters it is chiefly by one's own experience that one is best qualified to arrive at an approximately correct conclusion.

This brings me to the attitude adopted by so many who are prone to believe without examination, and who resent the findings of those who have examined.

They say in effect : " You do not answer this or explain that " ; and there are advanced for explanation illustrations of spirit power which are said to have been experienced or witnessed by themselves, or by others in whom they have the utmost confidence.

Now, what direct evidence have I that such-and-such a manifestation has happened under the exact conditions claimed for them ?

How can I furnish an explanation of what I myself have not witnessed ?

Not believing in the possibility of spirit manifestation, I cannot but assume that the alleged occurrence is a figment of fancy rather than an objective instance of reality.

I have yet to learn that it is possible to disprove a negative ; and, in my opinion, in furnishing an explanation of subjective phenomena of this description, I should be dealing with a purely negative proposition.

I would lay emphasis upon the fact that whilst I do not accept the phenomena ascribed to spirit power as being of the nature claimed for them, I in no way deny the existence of another world; this other world of my hope and belief, however, being of a character very different from that depicted by the credulous, unscrupulous, and unscientific.

Death is certain, and a life after death may be equally certain, but what so far is lacking is demonstrable proof thereof. It is not likely that proof will come through the agency of those who, on the one hand, seek to make money out of dupes, or, on the other hand, through those who are gratifying an abnormal mystical instinct.

I have always felt the spirits of the departed

must be too worthily occupied in the celestial sphere to which they have been translated to return to this world to indulge in physical antics, and gabble or scribble volumes of meaningless nonsense wholly unworthy or unbecoming of a celestial visitor of no matter what grade of spiritual development.

At the moment of writing I note the Kaiser has outstepped even himself in the matter of blasphemous assumptions, putting entirely in the shade the claims of the most outrageous amongst mediumistic impostors. This megalomaniac German Emperor now claims not only the certainty of the God of Battles being on the side of the Central Powers, but that the Almighty personally directs the Central Empire's affairs to the confusion and undoing of the Allies. The Kaiser, one may take it, in his disordered vision sees the Almighty fighting side by side with the Germanic forces in much the same way as the Romans saw Castor and Pollux and the ancient Egyptians their god Osiris. As with the pagans of old, the god of the Kaiser will be a material deity, with whom he is able to have direct communication.

It would, I fear, be as useless to argue with the German Kaiser on the subject of his hallucination as it would be to try to convince the minor vision-seers that the celestial beings with whom they claim to have established connection are mere figments of the imagination.

Prior to the claim advanced by the Kaiser, the greatest extent in the direction of blasphemy the most shameless amongst mortals had gone had been found in the outrageous assumption of an American medium that he had formed an Apostolic Circle for materialisations. I had attended a so-called " Classic Circle " ; but an Apostolic one ? No ! That was far too much for me !

.   .   .   .   .   .

The Kaiser is indeed a weird, complex character. He is mentally constructed on a plane different from that of any other of this world's inhabitants whom, as a psychologist, I have done myself the honour of studying. His colossal vanity is an outstanding feature, and his excessive touchiness another.

From the beginning I knew to the full that I had unconsciously made myself a *persona non grata* to his Majesty through operating with my " subjects " chiefly by contact with the left hand, thus making experiments of this kind with him, in consequence of his infirmity, far too conspicuous. I do—as in tests requiring the drawing of a picture thought of by the subject—take the right hand, unless, of course, the artist be left-handed ; but, as a general thing, I find it easier and more satisfactory to operate through the left hand.

After the Kaiser's blasphemous references to his celestial partnership, an experiment through his right hand, requiring me to depict on a drawing-board his conception of the celestial result he had in his mind, would, I fancy, produce a glorified portrait of himself, probably with heavenly wings, and certainly with a halo. In arriving at this conclusion, I am strengthened by the information which came to me on the occasion of his Majesty's visit to the Holy Land.   It was to the effect that it was with great difficulty he was prevented entering Jerusalem on an ass, and from essaying an ascension in a captive balloon which was to have been included in the baggage taken with him to the Holy Land.

I trust the Kaiser will do me the favour of reading this book.   Apart from the regulations prohibiting intercourse with the enemy in time of war, the conditions governing the receipt of a work by an author other than a German subject, by the Head of the Hohenzollerns, prohibits my sending him a copy.

Many crowned heads and other rulers have done me the honour of accepting copies of my works ; and, for my sins, may have read them. But the Kaiser, Wilhelm II., has not done me a similar honour.

On the publication of *A Thought-Reader's Thoughts* I sent a copy to Count Hatzfeldt, the German Ambassador in London, with the request that he would do me the favour of forwarding it to his Majesty for his gracious acceptance.   I was well acquainted with his Excellency, who was present on the occasion of my reading the thoughts of the Kaiser's grandfather, Wilhelm I., and he duly despatched the book to Berlin.   My King and Queen had been graciously pleased to accept a copy of it, and so had other august personages.   But his Majesty the German Emperor was not disposed to be similarly gracious.

Back came the book *unopened*, with the curt information that it was contrary to the rigid Prussian Court etiquette for his Majesty to accept the work of an author who was not a German. I called upon Count Hatzfeldt, and he explained to me that a foreign author must have the proposed presentation of his work made through his own Ambassador, resident in Berlin. Upon this I wrote to my Ambassador, who, in return, informed me that before he could submit my book for his Majesty's gracious acceptance I must get the permission of the Foreign Secretary in London for him (the Ambassador) to make the presentation.

Well, the red-tapeism of all this did not appeal to me. I decided that the Kaiser might get his copy—should he so desire—in his own way, and I retained the returned advance copy, bearing my autograph, as a memento of the divine restrictions that doth hedge in a Hohenzollern.

I had had a previous experience of the divinity that doth hedge in the cast-iron etiquette of Hohenzollernism. Prince George of Hohenzollern—the only member of the family, so far as I know, who had a weakness for spiritualism—had expressed a desire to receive me, and, accompanied by my secretary, a German-American, I attended at his palace at the hour appointed. My secretary, I noticed, was attired in evening dress, with a quantity of decorations—which he was rightly entitled to wear or otherwise—pinned to the left breast of his coat, whilst I was wearing a frock-coat. The *maréchal-en-suite* received us

with marked courtesy ; but there was a critical,
deprecating look in his eye as he took a from-
top-to-toe glance at my attire. He called my
secretary aside, and then it was politely pointed
out that my costume, however suitable it might
be for London, was not *de rigueur* in Berlin so
far as a member of the Royal House of Prussia
was concerned, and I was asked if I minded
returning to my hotel and exchanging it for a
more appropriate get-up.

I explained that I was dressed exactly as I
should have been had I been calling privately on
the Prince of Wales at Marlborough House, and
that, however much I wished to fit myself in
with the rigid demands of his Royal Highness,
I had a conscientious objection to appearing in
broad daylight in the garb of a waiter out on
a " beano." So, in the end, I returned to my
hotel without having an audience of the Prince,
whose *amour propre*, I was afterwards to learn,
had been greatly offended.[1]

[1] I would say that the strict Hohenzollern etiquette
governing male attire ruled at the Rumanian Court as well
as in Berlin. At an official reception accorded me at the
royal palace in Bukarest, I, on my arrival, discovered that,
whilst the ladies of the gathering were in morning dress—
hats and bonnets and all that sort of thing—the men were in
uniform or in evening dress. Back I rushed to my hotel to
change and to make myself duly presentable. This made me
late. On explaining matters to King Carol he graciously
remarked that, in my case, it didn't matter in the least ; and
Queen Marie (then Crown Princess) amiably added that people
were there to see what I was pleased to show them, and not
how I was dressed. King Carol, by the by, added the insignia
of *Officier of the Crown of Rumania* to the decorations I was
expected to wear on that occasion.

I am wondering if the Prince, on his translation to that other sphere where, according to the author of *Sherlock Holmes*, the inhabitants wear clothes, will insist upon presentations being made to him in the attire which whilst he was in earth life in Berlin was alone acceptable.

. . . . . .

I might mention that in connection with *A Thought-Reader's Thoughts* another odd thing happened. The book had been prohibited in Russia, and, together with other works of mine, was on the official black list. However, when the Tzar Alexander III. was one of the family party, on the occasion of the celebration of the King and Queen of Denmark's golden wedding, at Castle Bernstorff, near Copenhagen, an august lady, to whom I had given a copy on its publication, placed it on a table by his Majesty's bedside, so that he could read it at his leisure. I think he did so. Anyhow, he evinced considerable interest in my experiments, whatever he may have thought of my outspokenness in connection with Bureaucracy's misrule—an outspokenness which succeeded in getting the book black-listed. It was very thoughtful of the august lady in question to let the Tzar of All the Russias see with his own eyes what his underlings would not permit to enter any part of his vast dominions.

. . . . . .

Sir Arthur Conan Doyle has thought fit to rebuke me (and apparently those who think with me) for my levity. As I pointed out at the time in the *Daily Express* (a paper which, by the by, in connection with the craze has been on the side of sanity), I was entirely with him in agreeing that spiritualism has something more than its comic side. One cannot overlook the tragic side of the movement, with its grave risks of mental derangement and moral undoing. The craze is an unreal, unhealthy one, and the following of it furnishes neither compensation nor results.

If in this book I have been the means of making the more understandable what, to many, may hitherto have seemed inexplicable,—if I have brought home to others the unrealities, follies, and chicaneries of the whole business,—I shall indeed be glad. And if I can be of service to anyone in doubt or in search of a natural explanation of what may seem to be supernatural, I shall be still more glad.

For years past I have ceased to give public demonstrations on the subject ; but as they provide the means of bringing more directly home to people than any other method the falsity of the claims of the mediums and their dupes to the supernatural origin of certain demonstrable phenomena, I should be disposed to return to the platform to demonstrate in the cause of scientific truth, and at the same time benefit such charities as may feel disposed to make use of my services.

PRINTED IN GREAT BRITAIN BY NEILL AND CO., LTD., EDINBURGH.

For EU product safety concerns, contact us at Calle de José Abascal, 56–1°, 28003 Madrid, Spain or eugpsr@cambridge.org.

www.ingramcontent.com/pod-product-compliance
Ingram Content Group UK Ltd.
Pitfield, Milton Keynes, MK11 3LW, UK
UKHW010341140625
459647UK00010B/744